Date Due

	MAR 2 8 1973		

*The
Compleat
Manager*

David A. Emery

The Compleat Manager

**COMBINING THE HUMANISTIC
AND SCIENTIFIC APPROACHES
TO THE MANAGEMENT JOB**

McGRAW-HILL BOOK COMPANY

New York   St. Louis   San Francisco   Dusseldorf   London
Mexico   Panama   Sydney   Toronto

THE COMPLEAT MANAGER

Preface

ABOUT FIFTEEN YEARS AGO, at the American Management Association, I helped design a course in executive communication.
My contribution lay primarily in the psychological factors that
complicate matters between senders and receivers of information. The course seemed to help some managers identify causes
of confusion they experienced with associates.

But even at that time, I suspected there must be some other
critical variables. Why, for example, are some very poor com-
municators able to stimulate loyalty and high productivity?
Why do so many top executives appear to be poor listeners?
Why are so few communications experts offered top management
positions?

Years later, as an associate of the Kepner-Tregoe organization, I had the opportunity to study a logically developed set of concepts for dealing with managerial information. It became clear that unless a sound, systematic analysis of work requirements, resources, and problems has been made, all the "communications skill" in the world is unlikely to sustain productivity and morale for long.

Nevertheless, the *approach* to others does make a difference in the support they will give to objectives, plans, and analyses. The point was brought home with great force in recent workshops conducted by the National Training Laboratory.

This book seeks to understand and apply relationships between analytical procedures and motivational factors; between the rational and the emotional in man at work. It places a high value on an orderly, systematic approach to managing and at the same time recognizes that leading others is a highly personal matter in which individual differences must be utilized, not smothered.

In keeping with this conviction, recommendations are not offered as perfect patterns to be copied. Instead, they are intended as examples to help the reader understand and optimize his own approach to managing.

Personally, I have been greatly helped by Benjamin Tregoe, who started me thinking systematically about information processes. The urging of Ralph Baldwin and Richard Samson induced me to put some of my experience and ideas into writing. My family's patience and forbearance helped get the book finished.

D. A. Emery

Contents

Author to Reader
What This Book Will Do for You

ALL HUMANS have creative capacity and would like to express it in their work. All managers bear a responsibility for maintaining control over resources, particularly people. Whether these two facts operate in conflict or in concert depends largely on managerial method. In the name of control, a manager can stifle creativity, turn *off* motivation, and ignite resentment and resistance. But there are also methods of control that stimulate creativity, turn *on* motivation, earn deep appreciation, and still keep appropriate authority in the hands of the manager.

That's what this book is about. It is designed to help managers fulfill their responsibilities in ways that will release the resources of subordinates for the mutual benefit of the organization and the individuals. In today's world of nebulous values, challenging youth, and affluent society, this kind of managing will soon be an absolute necessity. Peaceful preservation of "the establishment" may very well depend upon it.

Self-improvement in this direction is a realistic goal for managers. Every manager's approach to control varies widely under the pressure of day-to-day activity. As the recommendations in this book are developed, I am sure you will find many things you have done, many things you intended to do, and some things you would like to try. "Improvement" won't represent a complete reversal in managerial style for most readers. It will be more a matter of smoother coordination and increased consistency. In some cases there will be very little change in specific behavior, but rather a deeper understanding of *why* an approach has been effective.

A good theory is one that works. Therefore, I have tried to translate every point of theory into one or more concrete recommendations for action. These should be viewed as examples rather than final prescriptions, however, for the following three reasons:

1. Basic and applied research on leadership and management style has not been able to identify a universally "best" approach to managerial leadership.

2. Even if a "best" approach were agreed upon, leadership style is so much a part of individual personality and emotional makeup it is unlikely that many could follow the "ideal" pattern with conviction or achieve credibility.

3. To change habits requires powerful self-motivation, which is most likely to be stimulated when one has been directly involved in designing the targets he hopes to hit.

This is the plan of the book: Assume the reader already has ideas about management and some experience with it; assume the reader has observed both effective and ineffective managerial behavior in himself and in others; assume he is highly motivated to build on his strengths and bury his weaknesses. The task of the book then reduces to two steps:

1. Help the reader *identify* his own strengths and weaknesses as a manager.

2. Offer a *method* that will help the reader improve on his own performance.

To be really helpful, this method will have to apply to a wide variety of managerial situations. It will also have to be focused on managing in tomorrow's environment, not just on the problems we face today.

These goals will be attacked in the following manner: In Part 1, some of the basic roadblocks to self-improvement and to helping others improve will be examined. In Part 2, systems will be presented for coordinating others effectively in the basic tasks that must be accomplished by all management teams. These include setting goals; stimulating innovation; evaluating alternatives; planning, organizing, and controlling; and analyzing deviations from plan.

First Recommendation: If you picked this book up for casual edification, put it down right now. The chapters that follow aren't just for reading, they're for *work*. To get the most for your effort, don't try to absorb it all at one sitting. On the contrary, the basic approach discussed here can become a lifelong aid to your self-development as a manager and executive.

*The
Compleat
Manager*

part **1**

*Getting Set
for Self-development*

chapter 1

Manage Your Learning Process

EFFICIENCY IS ALWAYS A PRIMARY OBJECTIVE in managing, so let's work on it from the very beginning. Certain things such as frame of mind, motivational pattern, surrounding situation, energy level, timing, and other factors can make a world of difference:

■ To your own learning efficiency

■ To your effectiveness as you help those who report to you in their development

Learning, like managing, can be done in a haphazard fashion or it can follow an orderly plan. This chapter aims to accelerate your learning as a manager by applying research findings from the psychology of learning.

Pardon Me, Dr. Pavlov

If you're a manager, you're probably in a hurry. Therefore, I'm going to raid the files of learned professors like Pavlov,[1] Thorndike,[2] Ebbinghaus,[3] Allport,[4] Köhler,[5] and others without even pausing to introduce you to the dogs, cats, rats, and graduate students whose patient suffering enabled their tormentors to learn about learning. Here, in brief, are some principles that accelerate learning and reduce forgetting.

Motivation: Key to All Learning

Motivation is the most important single factor in learning, inside the laboratory or outside in the "real" world. Rat or man, there isn't much interest in learning *which way to go* until there's a *desire to get somewhere.*

If you are a manager, or plan to be one, there's no question about your wanting to get somewhere! But there is a very real and important question about *why.* There are different kinds of motivational drives behind the desire to improve managerial performance,[6] and the particular mix makes a big difference in the ease, speed, and results of learning.

The first step in developing a management method is to identify the motives underlying the desire for improvement.[7] This is necessary for two reasons:

1. A management method cannot be divorced from the motivational pattern of those involved. The two must be compatible, since conflicts between *how* one makes decisions and *why* one makes them can foul up even the most highly developed method of managing.

For example, one highly directive manager who was encountering resistance to some of his orders thought he might be able to manipulate more smoothly by establishing a "permissive" atmosphere in staff meetings. He opened his next session with an invitation to "work this thing out together"; but when the suggestions were all in, he called his own shots as usual. His subordinates weren't fooled for a minute. They still disliked his need to dominate all decisions, but now they also began to question whether he could be trusted.

2. Once a pattern of motivation has been recognized, it can often be changed. In fact, it is almost certain to change to some degree as life advances and new experiences are encountered. Insight into motivation can help channel these changes to productive ends.

Intrinsic versus Means-end Motivation

The motives to analyze and improve one's management practices fall into two very different categories. The first, called "intrinsic motivation," is the drive that is stimulated by a profound interest in managing, as a challenging task.

The manager who is motivated by intrinsic drives is fascinated by different approaches to leadership, by factors that block communications, by "top-down" versus "bottom-up" definition of objectives, and by a host of other concepts that have been applied to managerial work. He would go on studying and trying to improve his performance as a manager even if he were assured there would never be any promotional or financial rewards.

On the other hand, "means-end motivation," as the term suggests, refers to the drive toward an activity that arises because the activity is seen as an effective means of achieving some further objective. There are managers, for example, who find no particular interest in the task of managing but who still work very hard at it because they desire recognition, authority, and more money. Perhaps the extreme case of means-end motivation is the individual who actively dislikes managing but still plugs away at it because he doesn't see any other way to get the things he wants.

Test Your Motivation to Manage

Identifying one's own motivational patterns isn't easy. It's worth trying, however, because any insight you gain will be a great support to your self-development. Here are some questions that should help you identify the basis of your interest in management:

1. If pay and hours were equal, which would you rather be?

   Doctor _____   Manager _____

2. Which article would you prefer to read?
   "How to Save 10 Percent on Your Income Tax" _____
   "Theory of Delegation" _____

3. Which would you rather be?
   Star athlete _____   Coach _____

4. If pay and promotion were equal, which would you prefer to manage?

   A smooth-running, experienced team _____

   Individuals with diverse backgrounds who never worked together before _____

5. Which manager do you consider has made the greatest contribution?

   One who, through careful application of proven procedures, netted significant cost-savings _____

   One who has developed a new approach to organizing his men, though efficiency has suffered considerably during the exploratory process _____

6. When you reach retirement, which would you prefer?
   To devote your full time to leisure-time activities _____

   To continue in some sort of part-time managerial capacity _____

In each question, a preference for the second alternative suggests that the respondent finds intrinsic rewards in managing. This doesn't rule out the probability that he also appreciates the extrinsic rewards successful management usually brings. It does, however, give him a leg up in the learning process. He will find information about management technique interesting in its own right and won't have to push himself in his self-development.

A frank recognition of predominantly means-end motivation is no ground for despair. Many of the world's most successful managers felt this way early in their careers. Yet they developed a fascination for managing as they gained experience. There's nothing like encountering and overcoming some tough problems to stimulate real interest in an activity.

Psychologists have studied this kind of motivational development at great length. There is difference of opinion as to exactly *why* motives change as time passes, but there is general agreement that an activity having only means-end motivational value at one point in life may take on intrinsic value later on.

From Job to Profession

Many people in all walks of life first entered into their line of work primarily in order to make a living. But in the course of performing their duties, they discovered facets of their work they hadn't seen before and that interested them. Once the snowball of intrinsic motivation gets under way, it gathers momentum. In some, it reaches the point where they virtually eat, sleep, and breathe their work. This is one of the marks of the professional in any line of work.

The stronger your present intrinsic interest in managing, the more fun you'll get out of working through this book. On the other hand, anyone who does work through this book—whatever his motives—is almost sure to increase his intrinsic interest in managing.

Executive Dropouts

A final warning about motivation. One of the causes for abandoned careers at middle age and beyond is the discovery that all the effort and self-sacrifice over the years wasn't really worth it. The individual finally realizes that managing "really isn't my cup of tea," and life is too short to pour his dearest resources into an activity toward which he doesn't feel intrinsically motivated.

Fortunately, our changing environment is making it much easier to avoid this nightmare. For young people, there has never been a time in the history of the world when the demand for people to perform so many different kinds of work was so great. And this variety of occupational choice is increasing day by day.[8]

For people who are already earning their living, conditions for switching to a different line of work have never been as favorable as they are today. The old concept of a single, lifelong career in one line of work has given way to the possibility of major shifts even at advanced ages. While the individual who finds his lifelong occupation when he is young is to be envied, in my opinion, most people no longer look askance at the person who changes. In fact, he is frequently admired because such moves usually involve considerable effort and risk.

Two psychological factors argue strongly for taking such a risk, if one's present work has come to look like a dead end:

1. One of the most destructive things for an individual's work motivation and total personality is to remain locked in on a task that appears meaningless. Experiments on boredom have shown that people committed to apparently meaningless tasks fall into nonconstructive and aggressive behavior in a matter of minutes.

2. As age advances, learning ability normally declines. On the other hand, if new learning challenges are taken on, one's learning ability can be maintained. When job interest sags,

one first loses the desire for improvement. A major change in work often revives interest, since it is almost certain to require renewed learning activity.

Other Psychological Factors in Learning

While motivation is the key to learning, the ease of learning and amount of retention are also strongly affected by other factors. Here are some recommendations that accelerate the learning process no matter what mixture of intrinsic and means-end motivation happens to support it:

1. *Watch the portions.* Learning is like eating, in some respects. People have different individual capacities, but there's a limit to what anyone can take to advantage in one meal. We all need time to digest. That's why learning should be "spaced," rather than a long, continuous cram session.

Psychologists have conducted experiments in which two equally qualified groups of students were given the same material to learn in the same *total* amount of time. One group did all their learning in one stretch, while the other broke the work up into several periods. When both groups were tested, the people whose learning had been spaced remembered much more.

This finding applies to the study of management in two ways. First, there's the matter of better retention. But much more important, the ideas you develop as you read this book won't really be *learned* until they have been *put into action.* Before you try to improve in many ways at once, remember the swimmer who tried to tighten up his kick, reduce his body roll, stretch out his arm reach, and put more snap into his breathing all at the same time. He almost drowned!

Take one idea at a time. Think about it. Compare it with your own experience and with what you've seen other managers do. If you find something worth trying, do so—with a step-by-step plan in mind. Then evaluate the results. If they are favorable, you may still want to check out the new approach again before going on to something else.

2. *Reinforce your learning.* The "curve of forgetting" is one of the best-documented findings of psychologists. It drops off steeply at first and then gradually levels off. Therefore, if full advantage is to be gained, a new concept should be applied *just as soon as possible after it is acquired.* This is the best known way to lick the curve of forgetting.

Your memory for newly learned material can be reinforced by reviewing the subject matter. Putting it into action is a much more powerful means of making it stick, however, because it adds so much meaning to the ideas.

3. *Look for relationships.* The psychologist Ebbinghaus, in order to have his subjects start on an equal footing, used meaningless nonsense syllables as subject matter for his experiments on learning. It's not surprising that what Ebbinghaus ended up studying was *forgetting.* For intelligent humans, nothing is harder to retain than an item unrelated to other experiences and principles.

As you work through the management principles in the chapters ahead, build relationships by making sure you see how they tie in with each other. Also, check how they fit in with, or perhaps are different from, ideas you already have. Wherever you find an apparent inconsistency, check it out. It may be a communication problem between the text and you, or it may be that the point in question needs to be tried out in order to be understood.

Since the real purpose here is to help you develop your *own* system for managing, none of the concepts covered in this book can be fully "related" until you have tested them through practical application. As you do this, with different concepts and in different situations, a set of guidelines will emerge that you know you can depend upon.

Critical Test

The most critical conceptual test you can apply to the management principles you develop is the test of *overall consistency*. The variety and complexity of situations and problems managers face, together with the nature of human learning processes, make a step-by-step approach necessary when self-improvement is the objective. However, as each new concept is considered, it should not only be looked at as a guide for dealing with a specific situation, but it should also be examined to see whether it fits in with the other approaches you have found to be effective.

In the end, *all* the ideas you develop and test must link up so there is no conflict between different individual ideas and so that when you look at all your ideas together they form a *unified, meaningful pattern*. When the way you deal with an individual's breach of discipline bears a clear-cut relationship to the way you set up a task force to tackle an R&D problem, then you are managing by *method*—not a hit or miss reaction to each situation as it comes along.

Ultimate Objective

Clearly, the ultimate in managing is to have *every* action you take directed by an inner understanding of how it fits into your total scheme of things as a manager: *your management process*. This is what this book aims to help you build.

While this task, if you stick to it, will be one of the most difficult you have ever undertaken, it should also be one of the most rewarding. The challenge of exploring and working out your own method for managing comes close to the challenge of living a meaningful life.

There are by-products, too. As your management decisions derive more and more from a *unified management process*, you will feel more and more secure in your knowledge that, come what may, you have done your best. Also, as you come to understand your own management process more fully, you will become more articulate in making it visible to others. This capability will be a great asset in persuading others to your point of view. A decision visibly derived from a logical, systematic structure of tested concepts is much harder to attack than one with no apparent backing other than the emotional conviction of the decider.

IN SUMMARY

The objective, then, is to build *your own* management process for analyzing information and dealing with people. Understanding your particular motivation for self-improvement is the starting point. Applying certain well-established principles of learning such as the step-by-step approach combined with immediate application will help you get there faster and with greater certainty.

chapter 2

Put Method
in Management Development

THERE ARE TWO CONTRASTING APPROACHES to learning and performing any human activity that requires skill:

1. The "natural," unconscious, intuitive way
2. The consciously planned, methodical, and systematic approach.

Tennis, for example, could be learned and played in a completely natural, unsystematic fashion. One could simply grab a racket, get out on the court, and start trying to hit the ball over the net. Without any teaching or detailed planning, one would naturally try to hit harder if the ball had been falling short; and after being repeatedly caught near the sidelines with the ball out of reach, one would tend to move to the center of the court after each stroke. Even with no conscious attention to anything other than trying to win, one's tennis would gradually improve. Some people prefer this kind of learning over a more disciplined approach.

But this natural way has serious limitations, even in activities involving a high degree of physical coordination. Its most serious drawback is that the ultimate level of skill attained falls far short of what can be achieved with a systematic approach. Pick any sport you wish. As systematic analysis and teaching have advanced, two things have resulted:

1. Performance by the champions has improved by leaps and bounds.

2. Many more people have been able to attain an intermediate-to-expert level of performance.

Steps That Trip

The limitations of natural learning become apparent when one considers the actual steps in this kind of learning process:

1. As the learner first moves into the activity, he adopts whatever style seems comfortable. Or he may try to imitate a more experienced performer.

2. This first style tends to be kept until serious difficulty is encountered.

3. Tripped up by trouble, the natural thing to do is to try different approaches, experimenting until one is hit upon that overcomes the immediate problem.

4. The successful pattern tends to get locked in and is repeated until further difficulty is encountered.

Note the inefficiencies in this learning procedure. Improvement is entirely dependent upon the kind of difficulties encountered, and the *rate* of learning is limited by the rate at which trouble happens to come up—and be noticed. Furthermore, the first approach found to overcome the problem will be adhered to, even though much better ways usually exist. It also frequently happens that the approach adopted to lick problem A is subsequently found to be in conflict with the approach adopted to lick problem B.

Apparently, the much-heralded "school of hard knocks" has some serious shortcomings as a learning system. Slowness and the likelihood of reinforcing bad habits are the major problems. It has also been found that trial-and-error learning is even more grossly inefficient when the activity involved is a more intellectual challenge, like managing people.

Systematic Approach

The fundamental difference between trial-and-error learning and a systematic approach is that the latter is a *consciously designed structure in which the timing and manner of introducing new elements is determined by their relationship to the overall long-range objectives of the total skill to be acquired.* This is the meaning of method in learning. It bears repeating and explanation because there are surprisingly many managers, executives, and even teachers who fail to apply a truly systematic approach in their work. So once again, *systematic method in work (including learning) means a step-by-step approach in which the sequence and content of each step has been determined by the relationship of that step to the activity as a whole.*

Tennis pros don't think of tennis in terms of scrambling over the court and somehow getting the ball back more often than the opponent, even though this is one definition of winning at tennis. What they have done over the years is to focus their attention on key elements of the game (the forehand, the backhand, the serve, etc.) with a conscious awareness of critical relationships:

1. The relative importance of these components to the game as a whole

2. The relationships that should exist between these major components

3. The detailed procedures found to be effective elements for strengthening major components and supporting their integration with the game as a whole

These same factors are fundamental in improving managerial performance. The study of management must begin by looking at the activity as a whole. Once an overview has been defined, major components must be identified and priorities established on the basis of the relative contribution of these components to the overall objectives of managing. Only then can an efficient job of improvement on specifics be done. There are two reasons for this:

1. Without a clear view of priorities, one runs the risk of devoting tremendous energy to trivialities.

2. Specific elements of any activity gain a large part of their meaning and value as a consequence of relationships to objectives, so progress is difficult to evaluate unless these relationships are kept in sight.

Executives Sense the Need for System

Here's some high-level support from the world of management. The 230 executives reporting to vice-presidents and higher company officials in one of the country's largest and most profitable corporations were asked to identify specific events that had resulted in unusually good or unusually poor consequences for the company. They were also questioned as to their views of what *caused* these events to be good or bad.

Over 800 critical incidents were discussed by the executives. Their views of causal factors were grouped into categories by the researchers. The overwhelming majority of these categories were items that centered around the *need for systematic procedures in management activities* such as analyzing problems, making decisions, and maintaining control. The other few cat-

egories dealt with breakdowns in communication, and stress
that often follows unsound procedures.

Similar studies have been conducted with lower levels of
management. They too have supported the good effects of
using a systematic approach, and have emphasized the cost
of a random attack.

Building Your Management Method: Step 1

The first step in building your own method of managing, or
in improving on the one you already have, is to make sure you
are clear on exactly what you mean by "managing." This is
vital, since the definition you settle on will determine your
whole outlook on the activity, the kinds of things you will regard as primary elements, the priorities you will assign to
them, your self-development activities, and your evaluations of
progress.

Just as research on managerial style has yet to identify a
generally accepted optimum pattern, so the students of management in general have yet to agree upon a single, universally applicable definition. While I intend to offer one at the
close of this chapter, I believe the best possible way to begin
work on a management process is to develop *your own definition* of management. It's worth the trouble because once
you've done it you will:

■ Really understand the definition
■ Believe in it
■ Have learned a lot in the process of working it out
■ Be motivated to derive consequences from the perspective
you have chosen
■ Be in a better position to evaluate the usefulness of the
definitions offered here

Defining something isn't easy, even when you are very familiar with what you want to define. "Definition," according to the dictionary, is the "explanation of meaning." But this doesn't exactly solve your problem since the "meaning" of an activity can be derived from its purposes, the activities involved, the actors involved, relationships to other activities, consequences of performing the activity, and other factors. Furthermore, no definition ever achieves a complete explanation of meaning, nor does it convey the same meaning to all users.

So strive for practicality, not perfection. Make your definition a *working* definition in the sense that it emphasizes what *you* regard as the important elements in your organizational environment for the immediate future. Here, as a basis for comparison, are several definitions that have been found useful by those who wrote them and useful to some others as well.

Sample Definitions [9-12]

Planning, Organizing, Integrating, and Measuring is the definition of managerial work adopted by the General Electric Company during its move to organizational decentralization. This emphasis was an attempt to stimulate managers at lower organization levels to assume a broader view of their responsibilities. ("Integrating" referred to a manager's role as a motivator and team builder. "Measuring" meant to add precision in control.)

Getting things done through others is a long-standing and popular way of looking at managing. It has served as the springboard for a wide variety of theories about the most effective ways to lead, motivate, persuade, and communicate in work situations.

Management is basically problem solving is an approach that underlies much of the recent work on logical processes for problem analysis and decision making. Some excellent work has been done in this area, but consequences for communication and motivation of people need to be developed more fully.

Process information to obtain results through people is my contribution. This definition recognizes that practical goals are the ultimate measure of managerial success. It also recognizes that systematic procedures for dealing with problems and decisions are essential. Finally, it stresses the fact that managerial effectiveness depends upon skill in communicating with those who will ultimately implement the managerial decisions.

Framework for the Book

The manager as an information processor and communicator is the context in which you will be encouraged to build your own management process. Examples of different managerial approaches to key information processing responsibilities will be compared to help you design the most effective approach for your work as a manager of problem solvers, innovators, decision makers, and controllers.

IN SUMMARY

This chapter has stressed the importance of a systematic approach to self-development of managerial skill. Working out *one's own* definition of management was recommended as a logical first step, since this can form a conceptual core to which all subsequent ideas should be related.

part **2**

*Managing Information
and People*

chapter 3

A Manager's
Information Process

IT TAKES A PROCESS TO BUILD A PROCESS! Once you've pinned
down a working definition of management, the next step is to
identify major elements or activities that are included in your
concept of managing. The definition you settled on should provide a lead to the elements you want to emphasize.

For example, using my definition (". . . process information
to obtain results through people"), a good first step is to think
through *what kinds of information* a manager has to process
and *to what purposes?* Once this has been done, you're in position to go for the real payoff question, *how* should these different kinds of information be processed in order to obtain the
best results through your people?

The following five categories represent one way of looking at the kinds of information managers must deal with. I have found this classification useful as a way to divide the mass of work managers do into portions that are small enough to think about in detail, and yet they still represent meaningful and significant pieces of managerial work. These portions also permit a study of important relationships that bind them together, as well as a study of the effects of how they are approached and executed upon people's motivation and productivity at work.[13]

1. *Set goals.* As used here, "goals" are things you *want* to attain but haven't yet determined *how* to attain. Larger share of the market, increased innovation, reduced costs, lower turnover, fewer rejects, more competitive spirit, and more teamwork are a few examples. Establishing targets such as these is obviously the first step, and a periodically recurring step, in any organizational management process.

Goal setting, and review, is the most important phase of any management process. All subsequent phases of managing depend on it for their success. This means not only *what* goals are selected, but the *method* that is used in making the selection. For example, *the role played by subordinates in identifying goals and establishing priorities probably has more to do with their long-run motivation and teamwork than any other single factor over which a manager has control.* Chapter 4 will deal exclusively with goal-setting technique.

2. *Develop alternatives.* Once goals have been set, it is necessary to consider ways of attaining them. Sometimes the paths are well established, and sometimes you have to break new ground. Even when there is a standard approach, you'll probably want to explore the possibility of better alternatives.

Developing alternatives is the creative phase of the management information process. Chapter 5 will examine methods for stimulating creativity in your people, since this kind of involvement affects the climate of groups and can produce valuable innovations for the business.

3. *Evaluate alternatives.* Decision making is one of man's most complex psychological processes. It is also one phase of managerial work bearing responsibility that cannot be delegated. Others may contribute to the decision-making process, but ultimate responsibility for the choice remains with the manager. To complicate matters further, good decisions not only have to be made, *they have to be sold.*

Chapter 6 will compare processes for evaluating alternatives when information of questionable reliability must be used. It will suggest techniques for involving others in the decision making in such a way that—

■ Better decisions will be made.

■ Implementation of the decisions is more likely to receive wholehearted support.

4. *Plan, organize, and control.* These three management activities deserve a chapter or a book apiece in terms of their technical complexity and the variety of procedural mechanics available for handling the masses of detail they encompass. They are lumped into one category here, because for our purposes they represent different aspects of a single, continuous process: the designed coordination of human and material resources for scheduled goal achievement. Our primary concern will be the relationships between *methods* of planning, organizing, and controlling, and the *motivation* of the people involved.

Chapter 7 will suggest methods of planning, organizing, and controlling that optimize human and material resources. Efficiency in communications will also be a major consideration at this point.

5. *Analyze deviations.* No matter how thorough the efforts at planning and control, deviations inevitably occur. When these deviations are negative, they represent problems. Some

very successful managers actually view themselves primarily as professional problem solvers. While there is much more to managing, problem solving is undoubtedly a major element. Outstanding performance at it has sent quite a few managers leapfrogging into executive positions.

Chapter 8 will present different approaches to problem solving under the most difficult conditions: when information is incomplete, some of it superfluous, all of it of doubtful reliability, and more than one person is involved. Suggestions will be made for dealing with situations in which others, perhaps in superior positions, have strong biases about the causes of problems you're trying to solve.

Closing the Circle

These five steps for processing managerial information form a logical and necessary sequence, illustrated below.

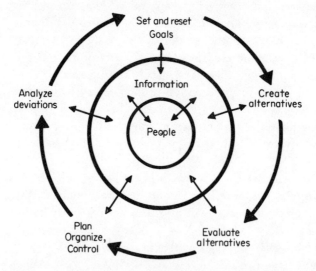

Even a preliminary look at the meaning of each step and its relationship to the steps that precede and follow it will show that any shift in the sequence would result in confusion and gross inefficiency.

Yet this is exactly what happens. For example, many a hectic search for alternatives has been conducted without a clearly specified and prioritized set of goals. Many a decision on a course of action has been made after only the briefest search for alternatives. Or to take an even bigger leap, many expensive attacks on problems have been carried out when a preliminary review of goal priorities would have indicated the entire problem wasn't worth the probable cost of solving it. Finally, it can also happen that new goals are set, or old ones revised, without sufficient understanding of the problems and the causes that motivated the upgrading of goals. Will higher bogeys increase production? It depends on why production never rose above its previous level. Will a cost-cutting program increase profits? It depends on why profits had sagged.

Thus we see that our five steps actually form a continuous cycle, in the sense that solving problems (step 5) usually leads to an upgrading or at least a sharpening of goals, which should stimulate a fresh search for better alternatives, and so on around the dynamic process.

Does this mean that procedurally, a manager should always be going around in circles? Not at all. Each step in the cycle, and each complete cycle, should result in improved performance. With improved performance comes higher goals, better alternatives, revised plans, etc. In other words, this never-ending cycling should really be conceived as a *continuing spiral of improvement*.

Where Are We?

The first purpose of identifying steps in the management process is to help you answer this question. I have witnessed so many staff meetings, so many conferences, so many extended task forces, where intelligent and industrious men were getting into deeper and deeper confusion—getting more and more frustrated with each other—primarily because no one had thought to get an agreement on exactly what they were trying to do.

When there is no mutual understanding as to what stage in the process of handling information the group should be tackling, it's not surprising to find one individual arguing for a new course of action while another is trying to pin down the cause of a problem—maybe not even the same problem the recommended action is supposed to cure! About the only thing you can count on is that tempers are rising and agreement, if reached, is more likely to be dictated than reasoned.

This state of affairs can be avoided in most cases. The way to do it is for the manager in charge to have a *visible* set of steps such as the five we have identified and make it his *first* order of business to establish where the group should dig in. To try to move ahead without common understanding on where you stand with respect to basic information process is just asking for trouble. If reaching agreement takes time, then that means the time was sorely needed. It also means that *much more* time would have been spent if the confusion hadn't been cleared up first.

Symptoms of Muddled Process

Relatively few people find it easy to be articulate about a management information process, even though many of them vaguely sense when things aren't proceeding in a logical manner. Here are some early warning signals of confusion over exactly *what* the team should be trying to accomplish at a particular point and *why:*

■ Lack of continuity in the discussion—people keep making different points rather than pursuing a single issue

■ When parties who disagree can't even agree on the cause of their disagreement

■ Wide divergence on agenda—some feeling it is time for decision, and others insisting more study is needed

■ Strong and continuous signs of frustration even though a wide range of alternatives is offered

■ Outright insistence that, "I just don't feel we're going about this in the right way!"

Whenever you encounter any of these reactions, back off from the immediate subject matter and run a quick check to make sure everyone at least agrees on "where we are" in the sense of some orderly approach to dealing with the situation at hand. The five steps in our management information process constitute one basis for sorting out where you are, and where you *should be*.[14]

Diagnostic Checkup on Process

There's an easy way to take a reading on the extent to which you and your team are already following an orderly procedure when you work together. Select someone that you consider a sensitive, objective observer and have him set up a chart like this:

Setting goals	Creating alternatives	Evaluating alternatives	Planning Organizing Controlling	Analyzing deviations

T

I

M

E

↓

↓

↓

Instruct him to be a silent observer in one of your staff meetings, simply putting an initial under the proper heading each time someone speaks or any time the same speaker changes the subject. Have him drop down a line for each new check so that a pattern can be traced over time.

Here, for example, is a brief part of a pattern that emerged from a meeting that had progress review as its announced objective.

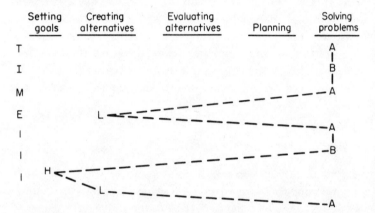

By drawing in the line after the meeting is over, it is possible to get a schematic view of how the discussion proceeded. Note that in this case, Art and Bob immediately plunged into an attempt to solve a pressing problem. Larry suggested a new approach, but it wasn't picked up. After a brief return to the problem, Hal raised a question about basic objectives. Then Larry reminded the group of his new idea. Etc., etc.

This kind of shorthand notation is easy to make and provides the basis for a very effective postmortem on the meeting. It will be immediately apparent to everyone whether the session could have been conducted more efficiently. If there is someone who continually tends to throw things off the track, this will also be visible.

In my experience, just a few applications of this kind of process recording does wonders for communications within a group. Individuals become much more self-disciplined in the timing and content of their contributions. Some of the load of continually checking on "where are we?" is removed from the manager's shoulders.[15]

Beyond Participation

These procedural recommendations apply whether your personal style of leading leans toward the more directive, authoritative approach or toward the less directive, participative technique. The need for a clear, mutual understanding on matters of procedure is a factor that stands with *any* kind of leadership style.

Research on leadership style and group atmosphere has shown that when a group loses sight of "where it is" (in a procedural sense) and what it is trying to accomplish, frustration and destructive behavior result with *both* "authoritarian" and "nondirective" leaders.[16] For example, promoters of "participative" management have been surprised by the fact that both in the laboratory and in industry, people are sometimes very productive under managers who use an "autocratic" approach. This productivity doesn't fit in with their theories about normal emotional response to an autocrat versus a leader who minimizes directing and invites maximum participation from subordinates.

I suggest that there are *other variables* operating that can be even more powerful than the boss's style of leadership. One of them is people's need to know *where they are, where they are going,* and *why.* This need for visible structure and rationale runs deep in most men. I believe it is the reason why many people prefer a manager who clarifies objectives and process steps, even if he is autocratic, to one who seeks a lot of participation but fails to get concurrence on exactly "where we are." [17]

Another Variable

In concluding this overview of a managerial information process and its relationship to leadership style, I want to make one point about work motivation and leadership that I consider absolutely fundamental:

I am in sharp disagreement with any conceptual scheme that suggests a split between "work" and "people." [18] To imply that effective management is a matter of balanced emphasis between the two so that neither is slighted, is most unfortunate in my opinion. People and work are inseparable elements of a dynamic relationship. The task of the manager is not to trade off between the two but to *unify* them in ways that accomplish the goals of the organization.

The true basis for "happy marriages" between people and work is *not* so much kind words, warm smiles, and promised security as it is the opportunity to take on a job that is viewed by the one who will perform it as:

■ *Important* to the operation, and recognized as such by others.

■ *Challenging*—there is a real possibility of failure within the desired limitations on resources.

■ *Doable*—from the beginning, success must be seen as probable, given a solid and consistent effort spiked by occasional all-out bursts.

■ *Fitting* the individual's own particular capabilities.

■ *Valuable* to mankind in general—the kind of thing he can talk about with pride to his children.

Give a man work like this and I claim you can virtually forget about "human relations," at least as long as nobody gets in his way! I also think you'll earn his loyalty whether your personal style happens to be warm, cold, participative, authoritarian, or any combination thereof.

The real value of a participative approach, in my opinion,

is that when combined with a sound information process, it can increase the chances of people finding themselves involved in tasks they regard as important, challenging, doable, fitting, and valuable. Whether it really helps depends upon the skill, sensitivity, and patience of the manager. Different techniques are required at different stages of the management information process, as different items become appropriate *and inappropriate* subjects for participative procedures.

In reference to our discussion of *intrinsic* versus *means-end* motivation, my point about participation is that it should *not* be regarded as an end in itself, of intrinsic value. In human organizations, the intrinsic value is a challenging activity that benefits the individual, the organization, and as many others as possible. Participation is only one means that may contribute to this end, depending on how it is managed.

Basic Concept

In the chapters that follow, managerial techniques involving a high degree of participation on the part of subordinates will be recommended. I want to make it clear right now that this is not done for the sake of stimulating participation. When it occurs, it will be because *at that particular point subordinates are judged to be the best source of information that is needed in order to construct an optimal approach to the work.* Conversely, when *other* parties, such as superiors, are judged to be better sources for particular information, they, and not subordinates, will be solicited.

If this sounds like a "cold" philosophy, it is not meant to be. On the contrary, it is my conviction that *human satisfaction from work depends primarily upon an efficient work information process.* Therefore, satisfaction will maximize as the work information process is optimized. If people are to enjoy important, challenging, doable, fitting, and valuable work, their inputs to the management information process must be controlled as much as possible through tested, systematic procedures. This is why the diagram on page 26 shows people and information as the dynamically interacting core of our management information process. People contribute information and are controlled by information. Hopefully, both functions will be carried out in an increasingly reliable and productive manner as we learn more about these processes.

IN SUMMARY

Chapter 3 has outlined five steps for processing managerial information. These procedural steps are believed to cover all the information any manager ever encounters, and are seen as forming a dynamic process that can guide a manager and his team to continuously improving performance.

The *first* item in improving performance is to agree on exactly "where we are," in terms of a management information process. Once this is clear, the team can dig into that particular step with all hands concentrating on the same task.

The next five chapters will discuss these five steps one at a time, examining techniques that can help a manager bring his people together into a team that sees its work as important, challenging, doable, fitting, and valuable.

chapter 4

Goal Setting

GOALS ARE THINGS YOU WANT TO ATTAIN but may not yet know *how* they are to be attained. They are the targets toward which all efforts of your organizational unit should be directed. Consequently, the effectiveness of your unit should be measured primarily in terms of its progress toward these targets. Goal setting is *clearly the most important responsibility of a manager*. Our discussion of goal setting is intended to help you develop your own best answers to these questions:

- Where should organizational goals come from?
- What are the relationships between individual goals and organizational goals?
- How can the power behind individual goals be harnessed to support organizational goals?

- Which is the best method for managers to use in goal setting and review?
- What are the consequences of goal-setting methods for productivity and morale?

Failure to take a close look at the commonplace is one of the common causes of inefficiency in human organizations. How many managers, for example, ever stop to ask, "Why are goals so important?" The answer seems to be self-evident, and yet a closer look at the question can give us leads toward a better definition of goals, deeper insight into the motivations of our people, techniques for building organizational loyalty, and a climate for appraisal that takes most of the pressure in that customarily unpleasant chore off the manager's shoulders.

Where There's Life, There Are Goals

The first thing to note about goals is that everyone has them; not just the brilliant, the ambitious, or the underprivileged. To have goals is almost synonymous with being alive. Conversely, it appears that removal of all goals can kill a man. Large numbers of American prisoners of war in Korea are reported to have died because their captors managed to take all sense of purpose away from them. The GIs nicknamed this death without apparent physical cause, "give-up-itis." A less extreme but much more common form is the reduced energy level and sense of futility that results from prolonged absence of challenging goals.

Another important characteristic of goals is that while most people have quite a number of them, we naturally set priorities so that only one or two dominate our motivation at any given time. Furthermore, when two opposing goals of nearly equal strength occupy our attention at the same time, the resulting conflict can cause tension, frustration, aggressive behavior, or even attempts to run out on the whole situation.

The origin of individual work goals is a complex affair,

which we won't try to push back any farther than to point out two probable sources:

1. Man's need to survive and improve his standard of living
2. His need to develop his natural capacities

What we have called means-end motivation includes the drive to work in order to survive and advance beyond mere survival. Intrinsic motivation in work would be the drive to perform and improve a craft just for the satisfaction of being able to do it well. With either source and type of motivation, there is one psychological aspect of goal setting by individuals that has important consequences for managing. This aspect is the fact that in our culture *most people seem to be more ready to believe and act on ideas they regard as their own, than the recommendations or commands of others.*

Of course there are wide individual and situational variations along this dimension. Still, most Americans place a high value on freedom and self-determination and want to see themselves as making their own decisions about goals at work or anywhere else they have a lot to gain or lose. Incidentally, this does not conflict with the common tendency to blame *others* when results based on personal goals turn out unfavorably.

Human goals are dynamic, in several senses:

1. As life advances, our goal priorities shift due to changes within us and changes in our environment.

2. For similar reasons, we also take on completely new goals and drop some of our old ones.

3. There are wide individual differences in specific goals and priorities.

4. Once a goal has been reached, the individual either reduces his goal-striving efforts or directs his attention toward different goals (shifts his priorities).

5. When people interact, as in a work group, the experience can impact their individual goals and priorities.

6. It is possible for people in a group to establish group goals that take precedence over their individual goals.

These observations about individual and group goals have so many profound implications for people's work motivation, continuity of service, creativity, and team cooperation that one point is clear: goal setting is no casual affair to be "gotten out of the way so we can get on with the job." Goal setting itself *is* a major element of managerial work. While the techniques we will discuss apply particularly to periodic reviews of goals, the manager's attention to goals should be a continuous, never-ending activity. In terms of our steps in a manager's information process, goals are:

- Stimulus for innovation
- Basis for the evaluation of alternatives
- Targets for plans and controls
- Criteria for prioritizing problems

Inputs for Organizational Goals[19]

There are two general sources of information for defining the goals of any organizational unit: sources "external" and "internal" to the unit itself. External sources include higher management, organizational units at the same level as the unit in question, and sources outside the company such as suppliers, customers, competitors, etc.

Jack Stringer, production manager of the surfboard department in Stoked Sports, Inc., will certainly get some of his directions for production section goals from his general manager. Another important source of data will be his counterpart over in marketing, who will have demand projections. The R&D manager, whose men have been testing a new collapsible model, has some recommendations that could add a whole new line to Jack's operation—or close him out completely! Another external factor affecting Jack's goals will be the quality and availability of the high-density foam he uses in his boards.

Internal sources include Jack's own ideas, together with

whatever ideas his people may have. Old Hans, the perfectionist down in shaping, has learned some things that ought to be reflected in next year's goals. Other technical specialists will have inputs, too.

To make the most of all this information and the motivations connected with it, Jack needs two kinds of procedural tools:

1. He needs an approach to *obtaining* the information that will net him his people's best thinking and leave them eager to support his final decisions on the section's goals and their priorities.

2. He needs a system for *organizing* the information he obtains so it can be reviewed, evaluated, and structured into a visible, workable set of guidelines for more specific plans and controls.

In short, Jack needs a procedure for managing the *human* aspect of goal setting, and he also needs a system for processing the *information* involved. The approaches he adopts for these two aspects of goal setting must support each other. Finally, since the processes adopted for goal setting are really just a subpart of the entire management process, they must also be compatible with all the other elements of that larger system. Specifically, if Jack sets up expectations by his goal-setting methods that are contradicted by his approach to control, he's likely to be worse off than if he had simply "played it by ear," without any conscious attempt to be systematic.

One Approach to Goal Setting

Jack Stringer knows what his general manager has in mind, and he makes it a point to check in with marketing, R&D, and the other departments on a regular basis. Naturally, he is constantly in close contact with Old Hans and the other craftsmen. In a sense, he represents the focal point of information that should set the goals for his department. Therefore, about the quickest and easiest way for Jack to set up his goals is to sit down and think it through for himself, perhaps with the aid of his assistant. Once he has reached his conclusions, he should present them to his people, explaining the reasoning behind his decisions.

This is a procedure used by many managers. Its success depends heavily upon the manager's own knowledge of the business, his familiarity with problems and procedural details within his own operation, and his ability to sell his conclusions to his people. It also depends upon the *process* he uses to organize all this information.

Here is a set of steps that have proven very helpful in assembling, sifting, and relating information for goal setting.

1. *List your likes.* This first identification of the things you would like your department to attain in the next operating period should be done in a very free and easy manner. Your chances of gathering in a list of creative, challenging goals are best if you *don't* try to be too realistic at this stage. Try to temporarily set aside what you know about limitations on resources, things the boss would never buy, and the attempts of others that failed. Let yourself dream a little; the whittling-down will be done at later stages of the goal-setting process. Now is your best chance to help the business break out of some of its long-standing limitations.

Jack Stringer, for example, might pull out all the stops on his imagination and come up with items like these in his first cut at department goals for the next year:

- Double our production.
- Cut costs in half.
- Hire three more shapers as good as Hans.
- Eliminate all health hazards.
- Automate the resin application process.
- Eliminate overtime.
- Develop a stronger, lighter foam.

■ Build a circular test tank with controlled, variable wave-size.

■ Develop a lightweight jet pack for powered boards.

■ Get R&D's collapsible model into production for next season's market.

Admittedly, some of Jack's ideas are pretty far out! Some are even beyond the present "state of the art"; some lie outside production's scope of responsibility; some probably have consequences that would be disastrous; some are financially unfeasible. But that's no problem at this point. In fact, something nearer the opposite is true: If your first cut at goals *doesn't* contain some wild and unrealistic-sounding ideas, you can be sure it has been a much too limited effort.

If ideas for goals you'd like to have your organization achieve are slow in coming or if you feel you must have overlooked some important ones, the standard checklist of *men, money, machines, materials, and time* can be helpful. Take these broad categories one at a time, and look for possible improvements in your operation from that point of view.

2. *Classify: Required versus Desired.* Now comes the first step in tying-down your *Likes* to the requirements and resource limitations of your operation. Go over your list of *Likes* and check each entry against the following criteria:

   a. Does it represent an absolute requirement, something that *must* be achieved within the next operating period?

   b. If not, is there some *lesser degree* of the item that should be required?

   c. Or is it an item that *could be dispensed with altogether,* if priorities make sacrifice necessary?

If a *Like* fits into *a* or *b,* it should be classed as *Required.* Otherwise, no matter how attractive, it should be classed only as *Desired.*

This classification is much more difficult than it appears at first glance. For one thing, there are very few "absolute requirements" in business. The ones that do exist tend to be taken for granted and frequently don't show up at all on managers' lists of goals, though they should. The reason they should is that the whole purpose of goal setting is to establish a sound set of criteria to guide managerial decision making. Stringer, for example, in his enthusiasm for new developments and leaps to new levels of efficiency, completely overlooked continuing requirements such as "retaining his present skilled personnel" and "maintaining quality standards on his current line." Items like these may not be glamorous; but they are important, especially since they are just the kind of thing that is likely to suffer in the rush toward innovation.

Another unavoidable complication in classifying Likes is that on closer scrutiny some of them will break down into two or more goals. These subdivisions may turn out to be two Required items, two Desired items, or some of each. When Jack Stringer takes a second look at his desire to get the new collapsible model into production in time for next season's market, he'll probably break it down into several items, like this:

- In production for next season's market (Required)
- In production three months prior to deadline (Desired)

This is because Jack has other projects he'd like to get under way. Also, he has learned to allow extra time for unforeseen contingencies, wherever possible.

A third complication at this stage of the analysis is that, in any list of Likes, some of the goals are sure to place limits on others, so that ultimately, trade-offs will have to be made. The main purpose of the third and fourth steps in goal setting is to provide as objective a guide as possible for these trade-offs.

3. *Specify: time, place, quantity.* Thinking along these lines will have begun in step 1 when items were first identified. It will have also been necessary in step 2 whenever single goals broke down into Required and Desired items. Now, however, it is time to do a complete job on every goal that is to be taken seriously. Exactly *when* is it to be completed? *Where* is the

completed work needed? *How many* items are to be included in the final accomplishment?

Jack had better think through right now what a realistic schedule for acquiring and breaking in additional shapers would be. This decision will be affected by his plans to increase production, his opinion of Old Hans's abilities as a trainer, and other considerations. If Jack is really serious about the test tank, *where* becomes a major consideration in judging feasibility. And when it comes to getting the new model into production, the goal has little meaning until quantities and delivery dates have been specified.

4. *Prioritize the desired.* There is no need to set priorities on Required goals, since things that *must* be accomplished should be regarded as all having equal and infinitely great priority. Desired goals are often of unequal importance, however, and need to have an indication of their relative significance attached to them. These priorities are a matter of your managerial judgment. Dollars are the ultimate common denominator of all managerial values, but some goals are almost impossible to express in terms of dollars. A simple way around this problem is to use a scale of numbers.

Here are two pointers about scaling that will help you select numbers representative of your judgments:

1. Use a scale that is large enough to express the full range of the differences you feel;

2. Don't use a scale that is so finely divided it implies precision beyond the capability of your judgments.

About as good a way as any to get a feel for a fitting scale of priority values is to select the goal you desire most and the one least important to you. Compare your judgments of these two and make sure your scale will at least permit a representation of this difference. Then pick two or three other goals and see if your tentative scale provides representative intermediate points for these items.

Stringer, for example, feels that automating the resin application process is his most important Desired goal, and that it's about five times as important as the elimination of overtime, his least important. Looking over some of the other items, Jack judges it will take more than five steps to rate the items as he sees them. So, he would probably use a ten-point scale.

Note that scaling is not the same as simple ranking. In priority scaling, it is perfectly possible to have several items with the same priority value (when there is no significant difference in their importance), and it is not necessary to use every number in the scale. To illustrate, here's the way Jack's classified, specified, and prioritized goals might look, in part:

Required Goals

1. New model: Ten per week by March 1.
2. Eliminate shaping bottleneck: Double capacity by November 1.
3. Safety: Improved venting for shaping and resin application by October 1.

Desired Goals

Priority	Item
10	Automate resin application by December 1.
8	Develop lighter foam with no loss in strength by June 1.
8	Triple shaping capacity by November 1.
5	Develop jet pack to fit standard board, cost $75 or less, January, 1969.

This list only includes Stringer's *innovation* goals. It does *not* represent *all* the things he wants to achieve or conditions he wants to maintain, by any means. For example, anything approaching a complete list would have to include items like "hold present accident rate," "hold present turnover rate," and "sustain production on our current lines" in the list of Required Goals. There would also be many additional entries in the Desired category, like "improve morale," "reduce scrap," "identify a potential backup for my position," and others.

I call attention to the incompleteness of Stringer's list because it's very natural to focus on change and improvement when listing goals—at the expense of standard conditions that are actually very important to preserve. If this omission goes unnoticed all the way through to the final choice of alternative means of implementation and on to the operational planning stage, some innovations may turn out to have costly consequences for less dramatic but much more essential elements of the operation. We will discuss some safeguards against such oversights in Chapter 6, "Evaluating Alternatives," and in Chapter 7, "Planning, Organizing, and Controlling."

How Many Goals?

There is no pat answer to this question, but there are some suggestive guidelines. No matter how many are listed, very few individuals can work effectively toward more than three to five challenging, high-priority goals in a year's time. This applies to highly trained technicians just as much as rank-and-file operators.

Groups can handle more but not nearly as many as three to five times the number of people in the group. If people are to function as a team, there must be overlap and identity in their goals. The scope of the goals, the kind of activities involved, the number of people, and many other factors make it impossible to offer numbers with assurance. My own observations suggest that ten to twelve high-priority goals are all most teams can handle. A good general principle is to *reduce* rather than expand the number of team goals in your final listing.

Something Missing

This four-step process can help a manager work his way from a cluster of vague wishes to a set of specific, prioritized targets at any organizational level in any kind of business. It is a tool to help locate and organize information into a visible, usable form. The next step would be to begin the search for alternative ways of achieving these goals. But before we move on, there is another whole aspect of goal setting to be dealt with: the *people* side.

A manager can *only perform as well as the people* who report to him. If you agree with this, then whatever process you consider for goal setting should be reviewed from this point of view: "Will this process, used as recommended, stimulate maximum support by my people?"

Looking over our observations about the conditions under which goals are most likely to be followed, as well as the dynamics of individual and group goals, there are good reasons to question whether Jack Stringer has done all he could. His goals appear to be constructive, challenging, and well organized; but the trouble is that they are in danger of remaining *his* goals, in the eyes of his people.

Another Approach

In the short run it will cost some time and patience, but in the long run there are tremendous gains to be made at each stage of the four-step goal-setting process if subordinates are directly involved.

Better Goals Accelerating technology makes it impossible for managers to keep up with all the detail under their authority. Even where basic knowledge is advancing slowly, subordinates' intimacy with the work is likely to produce ideas that may be lost unless they are drawn into the goal-setting process.

Old Hans, for example, may have some ideas about how to lighten a board that would cost a lot less than trying to develop a new foam. Also, he's probably found out some limitations of the present foam that could help specify the requirements of any replacement product. These money-saving ideas are there for the asking, but with some people, you do have to ask.

Fuller Support As we observed in our discussion of individual motivation, most people are more ready to support the goals they've had a hand in setting. This applies to individuals working in groups just as much as to a person working alone. In fact, *the consequences of prolonged subordination to unsupported goals are particularly serious where groups are concerned.* Reactions range from just going through the motions, up to outright rebellion including attacks upon the leader. On the other hand, when people in a group see themselves as sharing common goals they believe in, emotional involvement and work productivity can reach levels of effort far beyond a simple summation of their individual capabilities. While this kind of productivity *can* exist in support of dictated goals, it is much more likely to develop on a *sustained* basis when group members have had a major hand in setting the goals, so they regard the goals as *their own.*

More Insight Here is one payoff from involving subordinates in goal setting that has gone virtually unnoticed: by observing the kinds of suggestions his people make, the manager can gain a deeper understanding of their individual interests and values. This valuable information is there for the listening, because whether they are aware of it or not, people can't help projecting their personal work values and interests into their recommendations for goals of the unit. This information can help the manager in his tasks of:

■ *Organizing:* trying to fit people with work that holds *intrinsic* value for each individual.

■ *Controlling:* conducting periodic goal reviews in this manner provides a reliable reading of individual and group morale.

For example, if Jack Stringer asks Old Hans for his ideas about next year's goals, the shaper might very well recommend tighter controls on raw materials, or less frequent model changes. If Jack is really listening, this will remind him of Hans's perfectionism in work—a factor to keep in mind if any changes in the operation are contemplated or if he plans to use Hans as the trainer of new hires for the shaping shop. Hans's comment should also alert Jack to the possibility that the old shaper is *already* hurting some because of faulty materials and switches in his routine. While a department can't be designed around one man's idiosyncrasies, Hans is a valuable resource. Early awareness of his feelings may avoid a major blowup at a time when delay and adjustments would be much costlier.

The farther along you are in the normal cycle of a manager's information process, the more troublesome any major changes are likely to be. This is because of the resource commitments that have been made. If people are directly involved in goal setting and review, this kind of potential problem identification can begin when prevention and correction are easiest and cheapest. And if difficulties do develop in spite of everyone's participation, people are less likely to place all the blame on the manager. They are also more likely to pitch in and try to correct the problem as quickly as possible, since it represents a roadblock to *our* goals, not just to what *"he"* or *"the company"* wants.

Mutual Understanding   If teamwork begins at the original goal-setting stage, a solid basis for ironing out subsequent disagreements can be established. Different points of view on details of planning and controlling are bound to crop up, but they won't be hard to resolve if everyone is pulling toward the same goals. On the other hand, apparent agreement on methods will be short-lived if there are unexplored differences on fundamentals.

Performance appraisals are a case in point. These sensitive interviews are a good measure of how much real teamwork was involved in the original goal setting. Any managerial arbitrariness or haste in defining goals will now come home to roost with a vengeance. Where goals have not been met, the individual is much more likely to launch a direct attack on the goals as his defense. This is much less likely when he himself had a hand in establishing the original goals, and ample opportunity to question anything he considered unrealistic.

More Meaningful Work One of the unfortunate results of advancing technology has been to create jobs in which the individual worker only sees a small portion of a long, involved process. In situations like this, the only goals that have significant meaning are the ones that apply to the whole operation or at least to major phases of it. It is particularly important to get everyone involved in goal setting for operations or suboperations like this. Otherwise, their individual activities are likely to lose their apparent significance, especially under the grinding wear of repetition.

Mechanics

For effective involvement of your people in goal setting, have them participate in each of the four steps of our goal-setting information process. In order to determine how they can contribute most effectively, follow this general rule: *match the human process to the information process.* In other words, let the system that you consider most efficient for obtaining and organizing the information you need be your guide in making such decisions as:

■ Should I see them individually or as a group?

■ Is it better to get their ideas in writing or orally?

■ Can this be accomplished in a single session, or should I plan a series of meetings?

■ Should I offer my own ideas first, contribute them as we go along, or hold off until they've had maximum opportunity to have their say?

■ Are there any pitfalls in team goal setting, and what can I do to avoid them?

Here are some illustrative recommendations on how to organize people for goal setting if the four-step process described earlier in this chapter were to be applied:

1. *List your likes.* For your first freewheeling cut at challenging new goals get the whole team together at a time when they're as rested and relaxed as possible. Set aside at least two hours and protect them from interruptions. Do *not* encourage them to make advance preparations. The whole idea here is to have the group in a frame of mind where everyone feels free to throw out any idea he has without concern over his ability to defend it.

Probably the best method of stimulating a creative atmosphere is to open the meeting by explaining the process you intend to use for goal setting. If you have decided exactly how you're going to proceed, say so. If you're open to suggestions on method from the group, say so. The important thing is to *create a climate of trust* by telling exactly what your intentions are, and what is and is not expected of them. (Note that even when a freewheeling, highly participative approach to goal setting is used, someone must see to it that there is a clear understanding about general procedure. I regard this as an undelegable responsibility of the manager.)

Open meetings with all your subordinates are recommended rather than individual consultations or written proposals for the following reasons:

a. Years of experience with "brainstorming" have shown the value of group sessions where creativity is desired. A chain reaction in which one person's idea triggers another's will usually produce results that go beyond the range of individual attempts to break out of the ordinary.

b. This kind of approach is more likely to generate strong team spirit.

c. It's more fun this way. (Many managers are reluctant to associate work with "fun," but I think they make a big mistake. One of the surest ways to tell when you're getting intrinsic value out of your work is when it begins to be fun to do.)

The first team session at listing Likes is sure to start your people thinking along new lines. Since they will have had some good afterthoughts following the meeting, it's a good idea to begin step 2 by first asking if anyone has anything to add to the list. If this opens up a second flood of goals, don't be rigid about the agenda. Remember that it only takes one new idea to change the whole complexion of an operation. And even if nothing earthshaking comes forth, the enthusiasm shouldn't be stifled.

2. *Classify: Required versus Desired.* This is also best done with the entire team, in my opinion, since it is very important for everyone to understand why certain goals absolutely *must* be achieved and why in some cases other desired goals may have to be sacrificed to a degree in order to meet basic requirements. Any differences of opinion that arise at this stage should be resolved, whatever time it takes. If the reasons behind a goal classification are left unclear, full support for that goal is unlikely.

Some major requirements and limitations on department goals always come from higher management. As manager, it is your responsibility to communicate these to your people. The same is true for requirements and limitations that result from relationships between your department and other parallel functions. Many of these have already been defined by others or by necessity, and are not appropriate subjects for creativity. The only open question is how they can be implemented more effectively.

Then there are requirements and limitations that stem from the nature of operations and resources within your own department. As manager, you have a good picture of these. But your people should have an even better one, where their own work is concerned. Furthermore, they are much more likely to accept a locking-in on Required items and a paring-down of their Desired goals if they have done it themselves.

3. *Specify: time, place, quantity.* Now it is time to subdivide into smaller groups or task forces, sometimes consisting of only

one person. The purpose of this step is to pin down goals with as much precision as possible. In the interests of efficiency and accuracy, the task should be broken up and different goals reviewed by those who are in the best position to make realistic projections about them. When the various task forces have completed their work, these numbers and other specifics should be reported back to the entire team so that oversights can be corrected and the final step in goal setting and review can be undertaken.

4. *Prioritize the desired.* This should be done in a full team meeting if the value of the previous participation is to be realized. Since the priorities placed on goals have almost as much consequence for the work people will do as the content of those goals, it is essential that everyone be in on the process. This team approach to prioritizing does not preclude your determining priorities wherever you have information your subordinates lack. This, in fact, is your responsibility, and they will resent it if you fail to fulfill it. It is also expected of you because you are, after all, no outsider; you are the most important member of the team!

A Word of Warning

When people are invited to set goals for themselves, there is a common tendency to overestimate their capabilities. This overeagerness occurs both when individuals set their own goals and in group goal setting. There is real danger here because once it is discovered that standards are unrealistic, any of a number of things can happen:

1. Despondency may replace desire to succeed.

2. If the goals were set by the group, team spirit may break down.

3. Mutual recriminations among team members may do long-term damage to morale.

4. As manager, *you* may be blamed for "having led us into this mess."

Actually, as manager, it *is* your responsibility to maintain balance and realism in team goal setting. This requires skill and sensitivity, since you don't want to be in the position of inviting them to list challenging goals and then appear to throw a wet blanket on their ideas.

The secret, as before, is to stimulate *them* to do as much of the whittling-down as possible. The time to do it is in steps 2 and 3 (classifying and specifying). In keeping with this whole approach, use *questions* as much as possible:

> Do we really *have* to accomplish that, or is it just something we would like very much to accomplish?
>
> Is it realistic to think of completing that many by that time?
>
> If we commit ourselves to that and fail, what would the consequences be for those we supply? For our future appropriation requests?

There will, of course, be further opportunities to weed out unrealistic goals, particularly when you and your people get to the stage of trying to pin down *how* your goals will be achieved. The reason for trying to do it as early in the process as possible is to reduce wasted effort and disappointment.

IN SUMMARY

This chapter on goal setting has explored some fundamental characteristics of human goals, including some dynamics of individual and group goals. In order to utilize and control these forces, managers need a process for obtaining and organizing the information contained in goals. They also need methods for uniting their people into productive, realistic goal-setting teams. A four-step goal-setting approach has been developed that seeks to satisfy these two requirements and also produce challenging, specific, prioritized goals.

chapter 5

Creative Alternatives

"Creativity is for geniuses."

"Less than one in one hundred are truly creative."

"One thing about creativity: you either have it, or you don't!"

PRONOUNCEMENTS LIKE THESE are fairly typical of many people's attitude toward creativity. From their point of view, it is a rare gift that will probably never be understood and therefore cannot be taught.

Actually, there is mounting evidence to show that such assumptions are wrong in many respects:

1. Creativity, the development of novel approaches to accomplishing things, is extremely common.[20] There's hardly a

person who hasn't worked out some special ways of doing certain things that are different from the way he was taught to do them. We don't ordinarily regard them as such, but the way an individual ties a knot, dresses, speaks, or moves usually involves some degree of conscious or unconscious creativity. In a sense, creativity is as universal as individuality.

2. Creativity is *not* an "all-or-none" affair. It is a form of behavior that is exhibited in varying degrees. Hardly anyone totally lacks it, but there certainly are great individual differences. Some people seem to find it more comfortable to try to follow established patterns wherever they exist, while others take pleasure in trying to find a different, new way. You can observe this even in the way people drive!

3. Creativity *is* a highly understandable form of human behavior in many respects. We already know quite a bit about the environmental conditions under which it is most likely to appear, the characteristics of people who are above average in creative capacity, and the sequence of thought processes that help bring it on and then apply it most effectively.

4. Thanks to our knowledge about the conditions and process of creativity, it is possible to establish working conditions that will stimulate people to maximize their creative capacities. It is also possible to train people in systematic thought procedures that will increase the power of their own creative thinking. We will discuss some of these factors later in this chapter.

Symptoms of Creativity

Everyone possesses creative potential, but the extent to which it gets converted into action varies greatly from person to person. The following questions are designed to stimulate a review of how much your creativity gets expressed in everyday activities.

Of course answers to these questions do not depend upon

creativity alone. In each area, other circumstances and motivations can play a major role. Nevertheless, if a consistent pattern of response emerges, the chances are good that it is due in large part to creative urges.

In answering, if you find that you could go *either* way on some of the choices, pick the alternative you have followed more often. If it's still a toss-up, pick the one you would *prefer* to follow.

1. *On an auto trip with ample time, would you prefer to:*
    Stay on the route that you know from long experience leads directly to your destination?

    Try a road you've never taken before that may be longer but will probably still get you there in time?

2. *When using tools, as in hobbies or home repair, do you:*
    Generally use each tool the way it was designed to be used?

    Frequently find yourself using a tool in a completely different way than you were taught to use it?

3. *In the instances where you find yourself involved in highly repetitious activities, do you feel that you get bored and frustrated:*
    To about the same degree as others caught in the same situation?

    Much more rapidly and more intensely than most?

4. *As you look back over leisure-time activities in your life, have you tended to:*
    Focus your interests in one or two areas over long periods of time (five to ten years)?

    Take up quite a number of activities, moving on to another shortly after you have attained proficiency in one?

5. *Has your circle of acquaintances:*
    Remained fairly constant as long as you lived in any one location?

Expanded and shifted considerably, independently of whatever moving you may have done?

6. *Over the years, have you found yourself:*

Generally settling into established patterns in most areas of life?

Having difficulty shaking off your youthful restlessness and continuing to search for better solutions to life's frustrations and problems?

If most of your choices were for the first alternative on these questions, it does *not* mean you are devoid of creativity. On the other hand, if most of your answers were in the second category, you probably are well above average in readiness to put your creativity into action.

One point that is not likely to be visible in your responses to these items is the *change over the years* in the amount and kind of activity. To get a feel for this, go back over these items and compare your present responses with the way you think you would have answered them at *half* your present age.

Another point to be kept in mind is that many people deliberately channel almost all of their creative effort into a single line of activity, rather than display it in all aspects of their behavior. It may be some phase of their work or a hobby. The point is that such people follow routine approaches in other phases of life as a means of concentrating their creative energy where it has the most value to them.

In my experience, this kind of limited or "focused" creativity is the exception, not the rule. Creativity usually shows through in all the activities of the individual who cultivates it.

Misplaced Creativity

Creativity at the wrong time can be a problem. For an extreme case, consider a trapeze artist who comes up with a new catch-hold in the middle of his act! If you feel that's reaching too far, there are millions of more mundane examples where individuals fouled up expensive operations by trying what they thought was a "better way" when everything was geared to a standard procedure.

Misplaced creativity is worth examining not only because it is costly, but because analysis of the conditions that make it misplaced reveals essential elements of the management process within which creative thinking must be properly fitted. The helpfulness of new ways of doing things depends a lot on which stages of the management process have preceded the creation and which will follow.

For example, even very creative recommendations can be unnecessarily costly when they are developed before the *causes* of a malfunction have been identified. If your car fails to start on an unusually cold morning, it's natural to consider a tune-up or perhaps a new battery. Your children, being less inhibited by reality, may call for a new car or a move to Florida!

Creative or not, all these alternatives suffer from the same shortcoming: they were proposed *before* an investigation into the cause of the breakdown. This is inefficient—in personal matters or in business. It leaves open the possibility of much cheaper and more effective corrective action. In our example, all that was needed was to flush out the carburetor by adding one can of solvent with the next full tank of gas.

Referring to our information process cycle (page 26), it becomes apparent that there are a number of reasons for placing Create Alternatives where it is. The consequences of devoting time and other resources to this function at other stages of the management information process are worth considering.

Alternatives before Analysis?   Conjuring up creative alternatives may be fun, but we have just seen a simple example of how costly it can be when done before any systematic attempt to isolate causes. The "new way" can turn out to be a wonderful solution to a problem that didn't exist, while the real problem continues to foul things up.

Alternatives before Goal Setting? Even if problems and their probable causes have been pinned down as precisely as available information permits, a jump to corrective alternatives without first reviewing basic goals and goal priorities can be costly. The resources that get tied up in developing and testing new alternatives may be virtually wasted if higher-priority goals are outstanding.

At Stoked Sports, for example, the concept of a collapsible board developed from a problem that is clear to anyone who has ever handled a surfboard: their bulk makes extended portage on foot a problem (especially on a windy day) and special roof racks a necessity for safe auto transport. There's no ambiguity about the problem or its causes in this case, and a go-getter like Jack Stringer might be very likely to plunge right into a development program in hopes of coming up with a folding or even an inflatable model.

But would such a board sell in large quantity? Where is the market volume for surfboards? Among novices. Do novices buy surfboards only to surf? No. Status is a big factor. There are many more "highway surfers" (kids who drive around with boards on top their cars) than real surfers. And another factor: What will the sale of collapsible boards do to Stoked sales of roof racks?

Collapsible boards may be a great idea after all, but a review of fundamental goals and priorities is certainly in order before setting up a budget for the new project.

Alternatives after Planning? Since planning is the detailed scheduling of resources in order to implement a particular alternative that has been selected, to reopen the whole question of different alternatives at this point can bring things to a grinding halt. At the very least, it represents a distraction and therefore should be done only in the sense of developing alternate courses of action *in case the present one breaks down beyond feasible repair.* This identification of "backups" is an important element in the process of control and will be discussed in Chapter 7. It is, however, quite a different kind of search for alternatives, since at the control stage many more decisions have been made and resources committed than in the first cut at broad approaches or "strategies" for attaining goals.

Alternatives after Evaluation of Alternatives?   There are occasions when it *is* desirable to produce additional alternatives even after a first set has been created and evaluated. This is most likely to be the case when no single alternative from the first set has emerged as clearly superior to the others you have evaluated. Just when and how this recycling should be done will be discussed in the next chapter.

Involvement in Creativity

Now that we have this stage of the management information process securely locked in between Goal Setting and Review, and Evaluating Alternatives, the next step is to decide exactly *who* does it and *how* it should be done.

Creativity, we said, is for *everyone.* While different people have varying natural ability at different stages of the alternative development process, everyone should be included in some form or other, for exactly the same reasons we recommended team participation in goal setting. Applied here, these reasons are:

- *Better* alternatives
- Better *understanding* of alternatives
- More *support* of alternative
- Improved morale through *team* creativity

Furthermore, people who were involved in goal setting will certainly expect to have a hand in developing the means of implementing their goals.

How to Develop Creative Alternatives

The *process* of creativity is regarded by many as a psychological mystery. Actually, it is a highly understandable, logical procedure that can be described and controlled. In order to get a clear view of what the steps are in creativity and how they are related to each other, let's analyze the process as it happens in the field of architectural design. I pick this illustrative case because by its very nature it enables us to examine the development of a creative act in an explicit, visible context.

As you follow through the example, I want to call your attention to certain fundamental characteristics of creativity that will be illustrated:

1. Creativity is not a single, mysterious, mental explosion. It consists of a series of specific steps that can be understood and practiced by anyone motivated to do so.

2. Each step in the development of creative ideas involves well-known mental acts that we all have carried out millions of times.

3. The *sequential relationship* of the steps in creative thinking is extremely important in determining the value of the end product.

4. The judgment of whether a thought process led to a creative result depends more upon the nature of the *result* than on the nature of the *process*. If a new idea results, the thinking that produced it is likely to be considered creative; while if a very useful but already well-known idea results, the thinking is not likely to be labeled creative.

This is one of the major causes of all the confusion about creativity: the very same set of mental activities may produce creative alternatives in some cases and not in others. In fact the very same thought product will be regarded as highly creative by some people and not by others. It appears that up to now, creativity has been more a matter of perspective, than of process.

So let's see if we can take some of the mystery out of creativity, and in the process put ourselves in a position to produce more ideas that will strike others as highly creative!

Come Let Us Build Together

All attempts at creativity are triggered either by a specific problem or a general desire for improvement. In science, the "problem" that challenges the researcher is usually some gap in understanding. In architecture, the problem consists of a set of functional requirements that must be satisfied by a structure of pleasing appearance to be designed and constructed within budgetary limitations. In business and industry, the problem is some malfunction of people or machines, or both, that has serious cost consequences. Or it may be that no crisis exists and present objectives are being achieved, but someone decided to set some new goals.

Whether it is a problem or a new challenge, each of these situations points to the same basic need: to bridge a gap between a condition that exists now and a different one that is desired.

Step 1: Analysis of the Gap   If the stimulus to create new alternatives was a specific problem, then the first step toward better alternatives is as precise an analysis of what *caused* the problem as time and information permit. Detailed steps in problem analysis will be discussed in Chapter 8. For the present, let's just keep in mind that developing new alternatives to deal with a problem when the causes of the problem are unclear can be a very wasteful procedure. When the search for better alternatives grows out of a general desire for improvement, preliminary analysis is still called for. In this case, the

focus should be: What are the *differences* between the existing
and desired performance or condition?

I recently worked with an architect on the second floor plan
of a summer cottage. In response to some original discussion
of requirements, style preference and budget limitations, he
had produced a sketch along these lines:

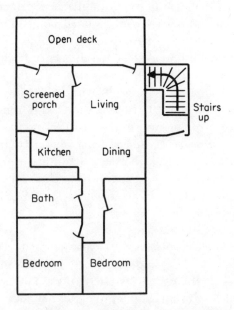

Although this plan provided that my living quarters would be
up where the view was best, there were aspects of it which I
didn't like: the extra enclosure for the stairwell added significant cost, and anyone coming from outside must cross the living room to reach the kitchen or other parts of the house. The
key *differences* between this preliminary plan and what I desired were *cost, distance* between entranceway and kitchen,
and *disruption* of stationary people by moving people.

Step 2: Definition of Requirements.   This follows directly from
the causes, or differences, that have been identified as responsi-

ble for the gap between existing conditions and what is desired. It may also include other items, such as things that are not required but are desired. As with goals (see Chapter 4), required and desired items should be specified (by item, place, time, and number). Desired items should also be prioritized to indicate their relative importance or value.

Notice that the identification of differences between the preliminary plan and what I really wanted points directly to requirements for better alternatives and also tends to force a more specific definition of these requirements. It now becomes apparent that what I really want is to have the entrance as close to the kitchen as possible without having my guests dropping into the soup! I also don't want kids from the beach tripping and dripping over guests just because the downstairs bathroom is already occupied. Some more careful thought about priorities revealed other facts about my requirements: I really didn't have to have a screened porch as long as the living room had plenty of screened windows, nor was I interested in a formal dining area.

Step 3: Search for Alternatives [20] [21]   The itemized, classified (required versus desired), and prioritized requirements now become guides in the search for alternatives. The mental process involved is association, the linking of one idea to another. A requirement suggests an alternative, and one alternative may suggest another. Quantity and variety should be the objective at this point, not quality. It has been found helpful to *withhold criticism* during this idea-producing stage. Another useful device is to work in groups, so one person's idea triggers associations in another's mind. This noncritical, group approach can produce a wide variety of alternatives and a sense of shared accomplishment when creative alternatives emerge.

Back at the drawing board, my architect and I decided to take one problem at a time and began looking for other places to put the stairs. With the reduced priority on a formal dining area, he suggested locating the stairs here, since this would be near the kitchen and also avoid the expensive additional small wing off the living room. In sketching a stairwell large enough to allow headroom for people starting up from the lower level, he first drew a rectangular well. This cut so far into the remaining living area that he modified the well into a triangular form.

Suddenly, the angular line of the stairwell suggested a whole new approach to the kitchen wall and sun deck, as shown below:

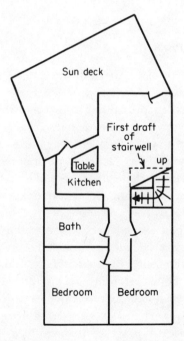

See what has happened? In the search for a better solution to certain functional requirements, my architect (aided by his eye for coherent design) hit upon a more effective, attractive, and less costly plan. The second plan provides direct access to the kitchen, leaves the living area undisturbed, and breaks away from the strict rectangularity of the first plan. It also gives me a much larger sun deck.

Admittedly, the relative attractiveness of the plans is a matter of taste. There is no question, however, that the second plan is a novel solution to some of the problems posed by the first. Note that this creative alternative *grew directly out of a systematic attempt to satisfy functional requirements that had been specified*. And yet, some summer tourist will probably pay tribute to the aesthetic originality of my house along these lines: "Man, I wonder what he was on when he took *that* trip!"

Creativity for Profit

The general steps of "Analysis of the Gap," "Definition of Requirements," and "Search for Alternatives" can be broken down into detailed procedural steps when the situation warrants it. This might be the case if repeated breakdowns of costly equipment occur. Or there may not have been any particular malfunction, just a desire to improve on a complex product or service, as there always should be.

For example, two young English aeronautical engineers recently came up with a new concept in commercial aviation equipment. Their work offers a fine example of systematic creativity that was carried out with sufficient precision to virtually dictate the choice of alternatives. Yet their end product —a most unorthodox ten-passenger aircraft called the Islander —represents a major departure from current aircraft design. Its wings are squared and straight across, it has a slab-sided instead of cylindrical fuselage, it has no aisle for passenger movement, it only goes one hundred and fifty miles an hour, and it can only fly one hour before going onto emergency reserve fuel.

Nevertheless, this funny-looking, extremely limited aircraft apparently possesses the capability of converting a marginal phase of commercial aviation into highly profitable operations. Let's see how they did it.

The Problem

The gross problem and its major causes were clear enough in this case. The fares that can be charged for short-haul passenger flights simply won't cover the high purchase and maintenance costs of modern aircraft and yield a profit. Still in gross terms, a much cheaper aircraft with much lower maintenance requirements would be a boon to the business.

Unfortunately, this level of analysis, though accurate, doesn't solve the problem. These points have been known for some time, yet no one has come up with equipment that would fill the bill. It took a more detailed analysis to isolate the key variables and suggest effective solutions. Here, using the Islander development as an example, are a set of steps that apply to a wide range of problems and situations. They are designed to:

1. *Identify essential functions* that are to be served by the equipment in question
2. *Evaluate present equipment* for its efficiency in serving these functions
3. *Suggest optimal approaches* to satisfying the most important functions

As we go through the detailed steps, I suggest that you select some piece of equipment with which you are familiar and apply the procedures outlined below to it. Who knows, maybe you will develop some creative alternatives of your own. At the very least, you'll gain a much better understanding of how the procedure operates. You may even see ways to improve on it.

Select the Item to Be Improved

Our creative Englishmen were probably correct in selecting the aircraft as the item most in need of optimization for the small airlines. It represents the airlines' *largest single cost item* by far, which is a prime factor for focusing creativity in business. It is also wise to begin by looking at a *whole* product or operation rather than selecting smaller subunits. There are two reasons for this:

1. Analysis that begins on larger units runs the least risk of overlooking the major possible functional improvements and cost savings.

2. Even when redesign of larger units proves unnecessary or unfeasible, effective analysis of smaller parts requires information about the larger unit of which the subunit is a component part.

As a general principle, the Englishmen should have begun their work with an overview of *all* aspects of short-haul airlines. It is conceivable they would have found other elements of the operations with potential cost-savings involving far less risk than developing a new aircraft, which required a $1.7 million capital loan and has not yet been sold in quantity.

Identify End-user Requirements

Having selected an area or a product for improvement, the next step is to list, classify, and prioritize the functional requirements of the item from the *ultimate user's point of view.* In most cases, this will be the customer. These requirements should be stated in *broad, general functional terms,* rather than referring to specific, customary means of satisfying the requirements.

In our example, identification of end-user functional requirements in general, functional terms could result in a listing of items like:

rapid transport   minimum effort
fifty to one hundred fifty miles   reasonable cost
  distance   adequate comfort
including luggage   maximum safety
minimum delays

Notice that even this listing doesn't suggest anything very different from the kind of service and aircraft currently available in typical short-haul operations (like Cleveland Lake Front to Detroit; or Waverly, Rhode Island to Block Island; or Fort Lauderdale to West End).

It's only when these broad requirements are specified in more detail and prioritized that suggestive possibilities begin to appear. For example, *how fast* is "rapid"? On a one-hundred-mile trip which would take three hours by limousine (including waiting and traffic delays), how much difference does it make to a customer whether his flying time is thirty minutes or forty-five minutes? Furthermore, what would his preference be if he knew the forty-five-minute flight was in an aircraft that is less likely to crash if an engine fails on takeoff (the most critical time for an engine failure)? Or consider the physical comfort factor: Does the passenger care to have more comfort and freedom of movement than he would have in a limousine, particularly when these limitations also add to his safety?

For the aircraft designer, each of these specifications on requirements opens up new design alternatives with different performance and cost consequences. The Englishmen ended up by producing a relatively slow, very short-range, very safe, nonplushy, and nonbeautiful aircraft that costs *less than half* of the nearest competition and will require much less maintenance. The key to their creativity was a thorough analysis of true functional requirements. In the process of doing this, they discovered that several customer needs were grossly *overserved* by present equipment, with tremendous cost consequences.

For example, all present equipment is capable of long-range

flight at high speed. But who needs it? Also, all present equipment has an aisle for passengers to walk up and down. But an aisle adds width to the fuselage, which adds drag and eats up power. And when passengers move about it shifts the plane's center of gravity, which adds to the pilot's control work and can be dangerous in a smaller plane. So the Islander has no aisle. Instead, it has enough doors to enable passengers to step directly up into their seats. This arrangement also makes loading and unloading faster and easier.

The Englishmen, recognizing the top priority of safety, engineered their plane so that at any speed the pilot can get it into the air, he has directional control if he loses an engine. A less critical, but very convenient, feature from the pilot's point of view is that he has less to remember in the Islander. The plane climbs at 85 mph, has a best engine-out speed of 85, flaps go on at 85, it glides at 85, and flare out for landing at 85!

There's a reason for recommending that your first listing be in broad, functional terms and then proceeding to specify these as precisely as possible. The purpose of the first listing is to break away as much as possible from the *present* methods of serving these functions. This increases the chances that completely different means of serving these functions will come to mind. On the other hand, a precise identification of just what is needed and how much or how little is needed helps point the way to the most efficient methods of serving these needs.

By the Numbers

Thought processes for producing better ideas can be organized into a visible structure that adds precision and reduces oversights. Here is one way to lay out information on requirements.

(See chart on page 71.)

By way of illustration, I have made entries from rough data

and judgments on typical short-haul aircraft now in use. Even though my entries lack precision and in some cases are debatable, I think some interesting and valid conclusions about opportunities for better alternatives can be drawn from this form of analysis.

The first place to look for leads is in the Cost column. In the case of an aircraft, all costs are so high that this doesn't

FUNCTIONAL REQUIREMENTS IDENTIFICATION CHART

PRODUCT or SERVICE: "Short-haul Aircraft"

	End-user Functions	Present Capability	Importance to User *	Presently Served †	Approximate Cost ‡
R E Q U I R E D	Safety	FAA Specifications	3	+ to ?	!
	Speed	300+ mph	2	!	!
	Distance	500+ miles	0 beyond destination	!	!
	Passengers	6–10	0 beyond own party	?	!
	Luggage	Same as airlines	3	+	+
D E S I R E D	Comfort	Luxurious	2	!	+
	Appearance	Elegant	1	!	!
	Servicing	Extensive	2	+	!
	Low cost	Expensive	3	−	!
	Visibility	Limited	2	?	−

* Weight from 3 to −3: "3" is top priority, "0" is of no value, "−3" is most undesirable.

† Code "!" if *overserved*, "+" if adequately served, "?" if marginally served, "−" if underserved, and "0" if unserved.

‡ Use dollars if possible. If not, estimate: "!" is great, "+" is significant, "−" is small.

help us much. However, if we compare the Cost entries with corresponding entries under Importance to User, some leads are likely to appear.

For example, Distance (beyond destination) and Appearance are both very expensive functions that are of little or no importance to customers. Speed, Comfort, and Servicing are also expensive functions that appear to be of secondary importance to customers. Servicing, in fact, becomes a *negative* factor when it causes departure delays. Indications from the chart are that cost-cutting any of these areas will make little or no difference to customers—particularly if top priority functions like safety and cost can be improved in the process.

Another way to focus on improvement opportunities is to compare the data under Importance to User with your judgments under Presently Served. Any overserved function is a natural area for cost-saving alternatives, particularly if the importance to the end user is not great. In our example, there are four *overserved* functions, and none of these are of great value to customers.

Our Englishmen probably did most of this analysis in their heads or in much greater quantitative detail. However, this format makes their thought processes visible, and in doing so it provides a structure that can develop leads to creative alternatives to a wide variety of products and services. It is interesting to note that the English engineers made their most creative and practical innovations exactly where the overserved and low end-user value but high-cost items appear in our chart.

If you'd like to test this approach on another example, perhaps one involving equipment more familiar to you, just fill in the chart using any current full-sized American automobile as the product. I predict that the analysis will verify why so many small, low-powered foreign cars are sold in this country in spite of Detroit's insistence that Americans don't go for those little bugs.

Move Over, Mr. Edison

To assist you in your next invention, I've compiled a list of Types of End-User Functions that products frequently serve— intentionally or not. The list certainly isn't complete, but it can help you to identify functions of an item that might otherwise be overlooked. Also, it will probably start you associating to produce others. Some of these unnoticed functions are just the place where cost-saving simplifications and customer-attracting features are waiting for somebody to find them. This list, you will note, contains both *functions* and *characteristics of functions:*

transport	speed	resistance to con-
protect	reliability	tamination
extend (power,	precision	temperature (idle,
ideas)	durability	operating)
inform	weight	safety
nourish	mobility	appearance
stimulate	strength (static,	sound
relax	operating)	smell
save labor	size	texture
preserve	maintainability	disposability

Human Resources for Creativity

There is no question in my mind that anyone who is willing to follow the procedures just illustrated can come up with creative alternatives. On the other hand, there is also no doubt that considerable individual differences in creative ability exist. As indicated at the beginning of the chapter, the differences I see are more in *phase* of creativity than in any overall presence or absence of the "gift."

People with strong analytical ability, for example, are naturally attracted to the problem-analysis and requirement-specification phases of creativity. Others, with high associative or "synthetic" ability find the search for alternatives the most rewarding phase. Still others, of a critical bent, come on strong when it's time to rule out unfeasible or undesirable alternatives that have been identified.

One of the most important skills in managing creativity is to organize the work so that people will be able to exploit their strengths and preferences. And if you have any doubts as to just what each individual's strengths are, the best way to optimize on this variable is to set it up so the people themselves have the freedom to move in and out of the activity as their interests dictate.

Clues to Creativity

There are a few indicators that can help a manager identify individuals who are likely to be above average in creative potential.

1. *Distaste for routine.* The individual who is continually trying to break away from standard procedures has one important motivational ingredient for creativity. Instead of trying to clamp down on it, why not try to harness it to a task he'll go for, such as developing new and better ways to accomplish some of the routines he abhors?

2. *Hypercritical.* It's easy to write this type of individual off as just "negative" by nature. Actually, he's a great resource for the first, analytical phase of creativity. His criticism can point out opportunities for innovation that more placid types would never see.

3. *Run-on talker.* People tend to turn away from the individual who, once started, is almost impossible to turn off. His insensitivity is a pain, all right, but his run-on conversation also indicates an associative ability that enables him to connect ideas more freely than most. This can be a great asset when it comes to the identification of alternatives. However,

you may want to have him work on this as a *one-man* task
force!

4. *Zany character.* Don't write off the oddball who rarely
appears to take anything seriously and who gets on some people's nerves with his endless antics. If all he does is tell old
jokes, his detractors may be right. But if his humor takes the
form of new twists, turning ideas around so people see the
funny side, he probably has natural gifts at breaking out of
standard frames of reference. This is a scarce commodity and
is an important element in identifying creative alternatives.

Note that many of these creative types are also potential
troublemakers. This is partly due to the greater frustration
they experience when confined to routine activity. When you
challenge such people to be creative, you kill two birds with
one stone; that is, you produce creative alternatives and reduce potential disciplinary problems.

Climate for Creativity [22]

In addition to being on the alert for individual differences
that suggest special ability in certain phases of the creative
process, there are things a manager can do that will stimulate
everyone to seek more creative solutions to problems. First,
build it into their job descriptions. Since motivation is a
major factor in all creativity, having the organization's desire
for it in black and white is one way of underscoring its value.
This entry won't have much meaning, however, unless the
subject is reviewed specifically and on a regular basis.

Second, *reward creative effort—including creative failures.*
Most cost-conscious managers will balk at this, but I still recommend it. Creativity will never become a way of life in a
unit where only the successes are rewarded and the failures are
punished. This seemingly logical approach puts the damper
on all but the greatest risk takers, who certainly don't have a

corner on all the good ideas. What it amounts to is that, if you really want creativity, *you* have to take a few risks, too. Nobody will expect you to pay off on failures the way you do for successes, but just a token reward for consistent effort will do wonders.

Third, *keep an "idea bank" for the whole group.* Creativity, once it starts flowing, won't be limited to today's problems. Some people will come up with better alternatives to old problems that have already been solved. Others will produce alternatives for problems that haven't happened, but might. Don't throw any of these out just because they don't deal with today's crisis, or because there is no crisis today. An idea bank, in the form of a special file opened to anyone in your unit, is one way of showing that you value new ideas anytime, on any subject.

Fourth, *encourage them to look at each other's activities.* If people get the idea that the only really welcome ideas are how they could do their *own* job better, they won't produce anywhere near the innovations that will pour forth if it is clear that there's open season on *all* aspects of the operation. This isn't just a question of defensiveness about one's own work and the kick of sharpshooting at others. The underlying reason for this recommendation is that for many people it's much easier to be creative about slightly unfamiliar situations than it is about things that have become routine.

Fifth, *welcome suggestions about better ways to manage* the operation. This is the real clincher for a subordinate. Once he sees that you even want his ideas about *your* activities, he'll know creativity is the order of everyday.

IN SUMMARY

This chapter has tried to make creativity an understandable, workable process. It examined some prevalent attitudes toward creativity that tend to scare off many who actually have the capability to contribute valuable innovations. It presented a set of symptomatic questions that help anyone identify creative potential in himself.

After placing creativity in its logical position within the management process, we dug into the underlying mental processes involved in creativity and set forth a systematic, step-by-step process for generating creative alternatives. This process was illustrated with examples in building construction and commercial aviation.

Finally, we turned to the matter of managing creativity. Methods of identifying individuals with creative potential and of motivating a team to greater and more consistent creative effort were discussed.

chapter 6

Evaluating Alternatives

MANAGEMENT LITERATURE AND MANAGEMENT SCHOOLS are breaking out all over with more and more sophisticated systems for evaluating alternatives. Decision analysis, decision tables, decision trees, and other approaches for classifying, prioritizing, quantifying, and comparing alternatives prior to decision offer a variety of tools to assist modern decision makers. The field has reached a level of technical sophistication that might lure high-speed learners right down into a maze of mechanics without ever pausing to mull over the basic mental processes involved in making a choice.

This could be dangerous. Personally, I believe that more poor decisions result from emotional bias, panic, and laziness than from lack of quantitative methods. If you have any doubts about this, test it against your personal experience in the following manner.

Look back, for a moment, and select what you regard as two or three of the major turning points in your adult life. A decision about moving, managing your personal finances, changing your line of work, or challenging a powerful authority are the kinds of things that might come to mind. The items you select may not have seemed like critical decisions at the time they were made, but from your *present* perspective, there should be no doubt that they did, in fact, have a tremendous influence on subsequent developments in your life.

From the turning points you've selected, focus on one that you would give almost anything to have a chance to reconsider and do over. (If none of them looks like this to you, then you're *really* in trouble.) The following questions should help you understand how and why you went the way you did at that critical point and what you might do differently in the future.

1. *Was it a fully conscious choice?* Surprisingly, many of life's most important decisions aren't really decided—they just "happen." An honest reexamination of critical turning points leaves many with the realization that they have drifted into, rather than decided, major alternatives that came up in their lives. This isn't only caused by mental laziness. *Many poor choices result from failure to recognize that a crucial decision is about to be made.* In other cases the importance is sensed, but somehow the person just couldn't get himself to step up to the decision and carry through a conscious, thorough, analytical evaluation.

2. *Did time pressures hamper you?* Most major decisions must be made within a limited time frame. Realizing that "no decision" usually constitutes a decision in itself, we often get panicky and plunge for the first alternative that looks attractive—or even just acceptable. Later on, perhaps as we

look back with regret, we realize that we could have been much more deliberate at the choice point than we were. *One of the first decisions to be made when approaching alternatives is how much time this decision is worth.* Once that judgment has been made, the reduced emotional tension from time pressure will free you for a more systematic evaluation.

3. *Was a third alternative really considered?* So many of life's major decisions are made with only two alternatives in sight. Often, all we look at are the obvious extremes: to do it, or not to do it; this way, or that. Sometimes we don't look beyond because we've actually already chosen, and the only reason we even identified a second possibility was so we could tell ourself (or someone else) that alternatives were considered. *If comparisons are worth making, always try to have at least three possibilities in sight before going into final elimination.* It's surprising how often the third alternative turns out to be the most desirable. This is because in the effort of identifying this additional possibility, we frequently manage to find something that avoids the worst features of the others.

4. *Were the circumstances emotionally loaded?* Completely aside from time pressures, there are very few important decisions that don't carry heavy emotional overtones. Fear of failure, eagerness for success, desire for approval, concern over consequences for others can make evaluation very difficult. To admonish someone to "be objective" in such circumstances is nonsense. Feelings can't be turned off at will. What can be done is to *help the decision maker be more aware of the intensity and direction of his feelings.* Then he's in a better position to factor them *consciously* into his evaluation.

5. *Did the original problem return to haunt you?* Most choices arise from a desire to overcome a problem and prevent its recurrence. Therefore, no matter how thoroughly the alternatives were evaluated, if major causes of the original problem remained hidden, there is always the chance that they will crop up again. In fact, *when these hidden causes involve deep-lying emotions, they are almost certain to recur.*

This point is worth special attention. Have you ever taken a close look at the careers of people who have risen high and then suffered a setback? You can bet on it that, as competent as they are, this wasn't their first failure. Buried back there under all that outstanding performance lie some problems whose basic causes involved strong, personal feelings. These feelings not only were a cause of the problem, they also were the cause of the individual wanting to push the problem behind him just as fast and quietly as possible. This is why some people's lives look like the same mistake repeated many times: poor job choices, or poor personal choices. Any one of those jobs, or relationships, might have been a success if only there had been a better understanding of the original problem.

6. *Did you lose sight of long-range goals?* Time is perhaps the trickiest dimension in decision making. The sharp contrast between the certainty we feel about the past versus the doubtful nature of the future makes it extremely difficult to balance priorities between short- and long-range goals. Probabilities and the reliability of information seem to change drastically as we mentally move out ahead of the present. The thoughtful decision maker can't help but wonder whether his subjective judgments about future probabilities have anything to do with reality. Caught in this quandary, *many people have a tendency not to put much store in the long range, and concentrate their thinking and their priorities on the immediate. This can be costly, for in some respects the future is as certain as the past.* For example, causes of past events are often unclear, but if you want a ten-year-old tree in ten years, it must be planted this year!

Two Fundamentals

The act of choosing is not an isolated event. It is part of an integrated process that goes back to an earlier plan, followed by unanticipated deviations from that plan, which in turn stimulated a desire to control such deviations in the future in order to achieve established or revised goals. Presumably more than one means of achieving the goals was identified, and as a result it is necessary to evaluate these alternatives before getting down to detailed planning on how to implement the most favorable alternative. That may seem like quite a mouthful, but after all, it's the whole managerial cycle in just two sentences!

The other basic point that strikes me about evaluation of alternatives is its tremendous vulnerability to emotional bias. Time pressures, old aches from past problems, desperate wishes for improvement, and other strong feelings can go to work on the vague and questionable data we have about the future in a way that makes systematic evaluation extremely difficult. This sets the challenge for the present chapter: to come up with practical methods for keeping these factors under reasonable control.

Our approach will be first to gain a deeper understanding of the psychological forces that operate when we evaluate alternatives and then to examine some specific procedural recommendations that help keep things under control. These procedural recommendations will deal with two aspects of decision making: the *methods of evaluation* to be used and the *people* to be involved.

Choice Psychological Factors [23]

The first step in controlling any situation is to understand it. In decision making, emotions are the primary basis of bias and the most difficult to control of all the factors that enter into the act of choosing. So let's take a look at some of these psychological forces in their simplest form, with the aim of understanding them at least to the point where they will be recognized whenever they crop up in the future—even if the context is much more complex.

The simplest and most attractive kind of choice people can

have is a decision between two highly desirable alternatives. The diagram below represents a person, or group, that has reached a choice point and must go either to the right or left in order to advance.

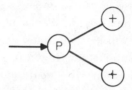

In this situation, both alternatives are of approximately equal value when viewed from a distance; each alternative becomes *more* attractive the closer one gets to it; selecting either alternative means giving up the other for the foreseeable future, and the person *does* want to get ahead.

What happens? One possibility is for the decision maker, in the process of taking a little closer look, to move toward one alternative, be struck by its increasing attractiveness, and zap in on it without ever really examining the other. Another possibility is for him to be temporarily stymied by the realization that to go either way means giving up an equally attractive alternative. So he hesitates, and the longer he hesitates the more unpleasant the whole situation becomes. This is because on the one hand he wants to move ahead, but on the other, he's afraid of giving up what might have been a better alternative. If the individual belongs to an organization where the accent is on aggressiveness and action, the very fact that he's slowing down on a decision makes the situation doubly bad. The psychological tension that builds up from such conflict can reach a point where the decision maker will lunge *either* way, just to get out of the bind. After it's all over, he may justify his behavior by the claim that "action is better than inaction."

But note that in neither of these situations did the decision maker conduct anything like a systematic evaluation, even though the elapsed time before moving in the second case might make it *look* like careful deliberation was under way. About the only thing a manager could do to tell what really went on would be to ask what factors were considered, and how they were evaluated. Even then, it sometimes takes very close listening to distinguish between predecision judgment and postdecision rationalization. When it is mainly rationalization, the giveaway will be that almost all the reported "evaluation" turns out to support the chosen alternative.

Incidentally, if we reverse the assumption about attractiveness increasing with proximity and make it *decrease* as the alternative is approached, the decision maker is almost sure to get in a high-tension bind from vacillation and procrastination. Each time he moves closer to one alternative, the other more distant one becomes relatively more attractive. As he oscillates, pressure for *some* kind of a decision builds up to the point where his final choice is more a matter of escape than evaluation.

Sugarcoated Pill

Here's another common choice situation that is seemingly simple but can develop some powerful emotional forces to blur evaluation.

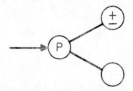

In this case, we have a decision between one alternative with both desirable and undesirable features and another with no clear-cut gains or losses. Again, we assume that selecting one means giving up the other. For some people, accepting a more challenging job with much greater exposure to top management, as opposed to remaining in one's present position, looks like this.

Now what happens? Tension is again likely to build up, this time caused by the conflict of driving and restraining forces as the decision maker approaches the positive-negative alternative. He may pass up an excellent opportunity just to escape the psychological pressure, which will increase the closer he gets to the source of conflict. Again, a decision has been made on emotional, rather than logical grounds.

Devil and the Deep Blue Sea

The most unpleasant set of alternatives to face is two negatives. An example might be a manager who has the choice of criticizing a popular and influential subordinate's marginal performance or avoiding the issue and having to live with the inadequate work and possible disrespect of other subordinates.

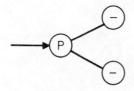

Here there's no escaping conflict, and procrastination will probably just make it worse. On the other hand, there is real danger in rushing ahead just to get an unpleasant decision out of the way.

The seasoned manager, approaching a situation like this, knows a certain amount of unpleasantness is inevitable. This awareness doesn't eliminate the conflict, but it does help him live with the tension while he carries out a thorough analysis of probable consequences of each alternative before deciding which way he'll go. In the case of the influential poor performer, the analysis might lead the manager to select a situation where the individual's poor work harmed the group's productivity, and then to conduct a *team* analysis of what caused the drop in total performance.

In a sense, this manager's analysis has led him to a *third* alternative, which is always desirable. Even when it does not become the final choice, its mere existence reduces the desperation that so often develops in an either-or situation.

Procrastination Can Pay

When a choice of alternatives looks like a toss-up, *time* (if the work permits, and you can stand the tension of a delayed decision) will usually change the picture. Even without additional research effort, new factors often come to light. At the very least, priorities shift. This is why it is so important to try to *distinguish between legitimate urgency for reaching a decision as opposed to pressures resulting from one's own emotional tensions.*

If there's doubt about this in your mind, one assist is to consult someone who knows the situation thoroughly, but has little to gain or lose from it. What you want his opinion on here is *not* what you should do, but *when* you should make this decision and *how much time* it is worth.

Methods for Orderly Evaluation

With three or more alternatives to evaluate and several factors that should be satisfied by the choice, it becomes difficult to make all the comparisons without some form of visible notation. Whatever form these decision-system records take, they all have the same basic purposes:

1. *To reduce omissions* of alternatives and important decision factors

2. *To increase precision* of judgment through refined prioritizing and quantification of factors

3. *To help convince* the decision makers and other responsible parties that a reliable evaluation has been made

Before moving into a brief survey of major approaches to

evaluating alternatives, one general recommendation must be emphasized: *try to keep the precision of your evaluation method in balance with the detail and reliability of the data available on your alternatives.* The danger is to assume that a decision system that produces lots of numbers necessarily produces a more trustworthy conclusion. The opposite can be true, if basic priorities have been distorted or if numerical values are based on shaky assumptions.

Another caution to be kept in mind is that when quantities with different degrees of reliability or precision are combined, the reliability or precision of the accumulated data may be no greater than the *least* precise element of critical data that went into the combination. It's like the strength of a chain with a weak link, except that when you combine information, the total may even be less trustworthy than the least reliable element. Some of the doubtful data may make other doubtful data even *more* doubtful.

The Pros and the Cons

One of the oldest and still most widely used methods for evaluating alternatives is to make lists of the good and bad features of each and then see which one has the most favorable balance.

GOOD features of this approach:

- Simple to understand
- Quick to apply
- Prompts search for good *and* bad factors
- Calls attention to *consequences*

BAD features of this approach:

- No visible definition of goals
- Mixes dimensions of comparison
- Implies judgments can be added, totals compared

On balance, is this a good method of evaluating alternatives? It can help identify factors to be considered in choices where the goals are few and very well known and where the probable contributions of the different alternatives toward these goals are so general in nature that it would be misleading to express them in even the simplest numerical ratings.

Decision Analysis

This is a considerably more complex and time-consuming method of evaluating alternatives, but it is much more reliable than listing and comparing pros and cons. It is adaptable to a wide range of choices, and can utilize information that is quantitatively precise or quite judgmental. There are many variations of decision analysis. The format I prefer is a slight variation on the one recommended by Kepner-Tregoe Associates in their management schools and in Chapter 10 of their book *The Rational Manager* published in 1965 in New York by McGraw-Hill.

The major advantage of decision analysis over many other approaches to evaluating alternatives is that it is built around a specific and explicit definition of goals. The *sequence* of events in a decision is very important in controlling against emotional bias and other contaminating factors. In decision analysis, the listing, defining, classifying, and prioritizing of goals is done *before* getting involved in the comparison of alternatives. By holding off any evaluation until after goals have been defined and committed to writing, one has a significantly better chance of having the final decision guided by a valid set of goals rather than some list that has been put together to help justify a foregone conclusion.

If a decision maker has been applying the management process recommended here—defining, classifying, and prioritizing goals before he even tries to develop alternative means of implementing them—he should be in the best possible position for reliable decision making. This is because by the time he approaches the choice point, *the decision maker should be committed to a specific set of goals*—long before he knows the particular alternatives he may be evaluating.

This doesn't make decision analysis bias-proof, but it does reduce one of the greatest dangers in all decision making: overlooking or distorting basic goals in one's eagerness to document a personal preference. Another advantage we shall see in decision analysis is the way it weeds out unfeasible alternatives early in the evaluation process. Any alternative that fails to satisfy Required goals is rejected without any evaluation against Desired goals. This is a great labor saver and permits a more thorough comparison of the feasible possibilities within the time available.

Finally, the Kepner-Tregoe form of decision analysis includes a systematic check for possible *negative* consequences of favored alternatives as the last step of evaluation. This is an excellent procedure for picking up inevitable oversights resulting from omitted goals and from looking primarily at the bright side of alternatives. This step is so important, in my view, that we will not only illustrate it in full procedural detail, but also give considerable thought to how you can use different people most effectively in identifying consequences. This is, after all, the last chance to identify major pitfalls before making the extensive commitments required to plan operational details.

Breaking the Bottleneck at Stoked

For an illustration of the decision analysis approach to evaluation alternatives, let's return to Jack Stringer's situation down in the Stoked Sports Company's production department. You may recall from our discussion of goal setting that one of Jack's highest-priority goals was to eliminate the surfboard production bottleneck caused by the shaping operation. Old Hans, who mans it, is one of the great board-shapers in the business, but he works at his own pace, and there's only one of him. As indicated in Stringer's innovation goals, Jack would like to triple the turnout of the shaping operation, and he regards at least doubling the output by November 1 as absolutely *required*.

Jack has identified three possible ways of licking his problem, but isn't at all sure which is the best.

1. Look outside for another first-rate shaper.
2. Train and promote one of the helpers.
3. Mechanize the shaping operation.

Each of these has some obvious positives and negatives aspects; but this is a big decision for Jack, with many long-range implications. He'd like to make sure that no major factors are overlooked and that other parts of the operation don't suffer inadvertently. To rely upon his own judgment, experience, and other intuitive processes looks a little risky.

So Jack moves into the first step of decision analysis, which is to list all the factors that he thinks should guide a decision of this kind. The kinds of considerations that come to mind are:

- Production quantity requirements
- Product quality
- Cost limitations
- Space limitations
- Impact on personnel
- Power, floor loading
- Future expansion capability

Note that none of these factors are news to a production manager. In fact, standard items like these ought to be on file at all times so they don't have to be thought up each time alternatives are faced. Instead, the manager who's "with it" will simply whip out his ever-ready checklist of decision factors for his area and get on with the evaluation. Ever-ready factor lists have two advantages:

1. Time saved
2. Less chance of bias from unintentional selection of factors favoring one of the alternatives

Ever-ready Priorities, Too

The closer one gets to a decision, the more powerful is the impact of emotional factors upon one's choice of alternatives. This is why the factors that guide a decision should be identified long in advance; if possible, in the cool that exists when no specific decision is even in sight. The same holds true for priorities placed on these factors. Once a particular alternative has begun to look attractive, it is amazing how priority values will shift and even disappear from a decision maker's perspective without his ever realizing what happened.

In his own best interests (and as part of his responsibility to Stoked Sports) Jack Stringer ought not only to have a list of decision factors all worked out in his top drawer; he should have these factors *classified* (Required versus Desired) and *prioritized* just like his innovation goals. Here's how part of Jack's decision-factor list might look:

Required Items

1. Double shaping productivity by November 1
2. Maintain product quality
3. Maintain present shaping cost per board

Priority	Desired Items
6	Fit in present shaping room
7	Meet power, floor-load limitations
9	No unfavorable impact on people
10	Future expansion capability

Note that these "ever-ready decision factors" have come to look very much like goals, both in content and in the way they have been classified and prioritized. That's not surprising because *a well-defined set of goals should be the basis of every significant choice of alternatives*. If important decisions aren't tied to basic goals, how can an organization ever hope to achieve the purposes for which it was created?

In fact, many of the decision factors used in evaluating alternatives will be taken directly from classified, prioritized departmental goals. Where differences come in, it will be because the goals could be specified in more detail in order to become more precise guides in certain kinds of decisions. For example, Stringer's general concern that any production change have no unfavorable impact on people, might be further specified into items like these:

- No threat to existing operators
- Meet Stoked safety requirements

Once specified, items like these will then require a fresh review with respect to Required versus Desired and priority values. In this case, Stringer would move the safety requirements factor up into the Required Items list, where its priority becomes infinite in the sense that any alternative failing to satisfy it would be rejected without further evaluation. The other item would receive a priority as a Desired Item.

Evaluation Matrix

The next step in decision analysis is to set up the choice alternatives and decision factors in an evaluation matrix. This is simply a device for making all the decision factors and alternatives visible, so none of the comparisons will be overlooked. The evaluation matrix of Stringer's choice might look like this:

DECISION FACTORS		ALTERNATIVES		
Required Items:		Hire	Train	Mechanize
Double productivity				
Maintain quality				
Hold present costs				
Stoked safety level				
Desired Items:	*Priority*			
No more space	6			
Power, floor load	7			
Future expansion	10			
Least threat	8			

Now Jack is ready to begin his actual evaluation. First comes the checkoff to see which alternatives pass the Required factors. Jack's judgments are shown by his entries under each alternative opposite the Required factors:

DECISION FACTORS	ALTERNATIVES		
Required Items:	Hire	Train	Mechanize
Double productivity	Okay	?	Okay
Maintain quality	Okay	?	?
Hold present costs	Okay	Okay	Okay
Stoked safety level	Okay	Okay	?

This first run-through of his alternatives against the Required factors, though done very quickly, may have saved Jack a lot of time. If a little checking confirms his doubts about training a helper and mechanization, then the decision is made, and no further evaluation is necessary.

Jack verified that the new mechanical shaper can (contrary to Old Hans's claims) shape top quality boards and that it is a well-guarded and vented machine. On the other hand, a close look at their past performance made it look extremely unlikely that either of the helpers could come anywhere Old Hans's quality level by November or even by the end of the year. This narrows Jack's alternatives to two, and leaves the decision to the Desired factors.

The procedure here is to consider each factor, one at a time, and ask, "Which of the available alternatives satisfies this factor best?" Whichever one does, receives top score. The remaining alternatives are then scored proportionately, to reflect how well (or poorly) they satisfy this same factor when compared to the alternative that satisfies it best.

For example, Jack Stringer, considering his space limitations, decided that adding a new shaper would not require as much additional space as installing the shaping machine. Accordingly, he gave his top score of 5 to the "hire" alternative, and only a 2 under "mechanize." The scale of numbers used in these ratings should be guided by the same judgmental criteria used in selecting the numbers for any numerical ratings:

1. Use a scale large enough to express the differences you can judge.

2. Limit the size of your scale so it doesn't imply greater precision than the data you are judging permits.

In this case, since he is only comparing two alternatives, Jack feels that a five-point scale can reflect all the differences he is likely to see.

Using this same comparative procedure, Jack enters his judgments on the remaining factors:

Desired Items:	Priority	(Hire)	(Mechanize)
No more space	6	5	2
Power, floor load	7	5	1
Future expansion	10	2	5
Least threat	8	5	4

Jack had considerable difficulty deciding which alternative offered the least threat to his existing work force. On one hand, the threat of mechanization might upset them, but they might also resent having a skilled man brought in "over their heads" instead of promoting from within. If these alternatives had been a standoff on the threat factor, Jack might just as well have dropped the entire question of threat from his evaluation matrix, since tie scores have no effect on the decision.

Once these judgments have been entered, Jack is ready to integrate his long-standing judgments of priorities with his current comparisons of alternatives against factors. This is done by multiplying the various scores by the priority values, as shown below.

Desired Items:	Priority	(Hire)	(Mechanize)
No more space	6	5×6= 30	2×6= 12
Power, floor load	7	5×7= 35	1×7= 7
Future expansion	10	2×10= 20	5×10= 50
Least threat	8	5×8= 40	4×8= 32
		125	101

The sums of these products indicate to Jack that, on balance, there appears to be a slight superiority of hiring a new shaper over installing a shaping machine when only these four factors are considered. Note, however, that a minor difference in scoring or in prioritizing could have eliminated or even reversed the trend.

Even if the score had been 200 to 100 in favor of hiring a new shaper, Jack Stringer would have involved himself and his people in needless risk had he made the decision on this basis alone. A final, major step remains in decision analysis that can reverse the strongest trends. Even when no reversal results, major savings in future planning and problem solving usually follow its application.

Pinpointing Pitfalls

The *purpose* of this final step in decision analysis is to try to anticipate major pitfalls in an alternative *before there has been any commitment* to follow that particular course of action. The result of potential problem analysis may be to:

- Totally reject the alternative in question
- Radically alter its manner of implementation
- Help establish remedial capability in case the anticipated difficulties actually develop

The *method* for quick but penetrating potential problem analysis involves three steps:

1. *Target the top contender.* Since the greatest danger at this stage is to sell yourself (and others) an alternative that has already begun to look attractive, this is the one to shoot at first. Stringer, for example, is almost ready to place an ad for shapers. Now is the time to take a very critical look at the whole scheme.

2. *Try your best to shoot it down.* Armed with the certainty that no alternative is perfect, try your best to anticipate *what could go wrong* with the one you favor. Stringer may simply

be unable to *find* another shaper as good as Hans. Hans may resent the addition. The new man may stay just long enough to steal Stoked's special techniques. Etc., etc.

3. *Integrate the remains.* What you have actually done, from your critical perspective, is to generate some additional factors that should help guide your decision. These can be translated into your evaluation matrix so their possible impact can be judged in relation to your other evaluations. For example, Jack's concern over finding another shaper raises the general question of "availability"; his fear of friction between Hans and the new man may change his priority and/or scoring of the "threat to existing personnel" factor; the final item may suggest a general "security" factor. Altogether, these might produce the following changes and additions to Jack's matrix.

Desired Items:	*Priority*	(Hire)	(Mechanize)
No more space	6	5×6= 30	2×6= 12
Power, floor load	7	5×7= 35	1×7= 7
Future expansion	10	2×10= 20	5×10= 50
Least threat	(8) 10	3×10= 30	5×10= 50
Availability	7	3×7= 21	5×7= 35
Least security risk	5	3×5= 15	5×5= 25
		151	179

Now it appears that Stringer's potential problem analysis has reversed his original preference, though the margin of difference is unimpressive. Impressive or not, before he starts shopping for a shaping machine, Jack will do well to conduct a potential problem analysis on *that* alternative, too. If done in an honestly critical attitude, new evaluation factors are sure to emerge.

Help from a Pro

Have you ever seen an organization that didn't have at least one member who made it his business to focus on the *negative* and make a fuss about it? These self-styled critics may be a pain in the aspirations of many more constructively oriented individuals, but they can serve you well when it comes to potential problem analysis. This is the time to call in your "professional" critic and turn him loose on your favored alternative. If he's particularly negative in his outlook, let him know that you think pretty highly of the alternative: it'll stimulate him to even greater critical effort. And when he's submitted his ideas, don't forget to show your appreciation. Underneath that caustic exterior there's almost certain to be a tender, uncertain individual who has been using desperate means to get the attention he craves.

Make Evaluation a Team Play

Choice situations like this shouldn't be kept to yourself. If time is so pressing you feel you can't afford to get the others involved, then you'd better review priorities. Decisions on a major alternative should *never* be made in a hurry. When time is short, it's much better to abbreviate the process than the participation, for two major reasons.

1. Your associates and subordinates will have crucial inputs for both the definition of decision factors and identification of potential problems.

2. They, not you, are the ones who will ultimately implement the chosen alternative, so it's essential that they get the best possible understanding of it and support it from the very outset.

If you've been applying the management process recommended here, your people will already be well prepared to help you in choosing alternatives. Their earlier participation in goal setting and the identification of alternatives will have left them informed on the decision factors and involved in the question of which alternative will finally win out. Furthermore, their closeness to certain elements of the work makes them excellent sources of information on specifics when it comes to comparing alternatives against factors and projecting what could go wrong with a favored alternative. Perhaps most important of all: if the final decision has been *our* decision, rather than just *his,* tremendous additional motivational forces are automatically cranked in to help prove through successful results that it was a *good* decision.

This last point has been proven time and again in controlled experiments with groups. Whether the alternative under consideration was inherently appealing to the group members or not, there was *always* much more follow-up action when the group members were involved in making the decision than when some expert—no matter how knowledgeable or silver-tongued—tried to persuade the others. Expectant mothers stuck to their diets; people ate more "glandular" meat during a period of meat shortage; people exhibited more tolerance toward members of differing religious and racial groups —all under the power of a group decision with its much greater sense of personal commitment.

Contribution without Kaffee Klatsch

Participation in choice of alternatives need not imply an endless round of committee meetings. The trick for stimulating a sense of involvement without tying everybody up in long discussions is to schedule the right people at the right stage of the choice process. Here is a suggested schedule showing the process stage, *who* should be involved, and just *what* should be accomplished.

1. *Identify decision factors.* At this initial stage of a major choice it's a good idea to have the whole gang get together so everyone gets firsthand knowledge of what's going on. It provides a good opportunity for reviewing relevant goals and soliciting their ideas for additional or more specific decision factors that ought to be applied in making the choice. If the session starts to drag on, you can always direct them to write

up their ideas and turn them in to you, or to a "Factor Review Task Force" consisting of three to four people most directly affected by the decision. You may want to appoint this key unit or have them nominated with your approval by the entire group.

2. *Classify and prioritize factors.* This is work for key people who know the background of the decision and have a strong sense of responsibility for the entire operation. If your Factor Review Task Force meets these criteria, they are in an excellent position to evaluate which factors are required and which ones are only desired, and to recommend priority ratings for the desired items. None of these recommendations should be finalized without your approval.

3. *Check alternatives against required factors.* All your people will appreciate being in on this step, since some crucial decisions affecting everyone are likely to be made. You should manage the discussion, but there's no need for you to initiate the decisions. *Approval* is your prerogative and responsibility. If you have checked out the job done by the Factor Review Task Force on defining required factors, you have nothing to fear from a free and open discussion of which alternatives do or don't satisfy these key factors and why.

4. *Evaluate alternatives against desired factors.* This is a complex and time-consuming job that can only be done efficiently by a small group who have intimate knowledge of current operations, the alternatives, and the evaluation factors. The Factor Review Task Force may be just the right team, or you may want to shift the membership to reflect maximum knowledge of the remaining alternatives (after eliminations of step 3, above). The judgments of this stage should be reported to and reviewed by the entire group that will be affected by the decision. Both the evaluation process and its reporting require close supervision by you. In the final reporting session, take up each judgment at a time, holding the exposure of overall sums and results to the very end.

5. *Potential problem analysis.* Now is the time to bring in

"fresh" personnel: fresh in the sense of being relatively new to the problem and of having no reluctance to criticize the alternatives that have emerged thus far. At least three or four people should share this devil's advocate task, and it's even better if you can set up two or three of these critical groups to carry out their work in parallel, independently of each other. Be sure they understand that the more they can find wrong with present front-running alternatives, the greater service they will have rendered the whole operation.

6. *The final decision.* After all the evaluation, potential problem analysis, and recycling through the decision process has been completed, your entire team still deserves a final, full-scale report on the entire evaluation of the alternatives. If they feel free to question and criticize, this group review will not only help get the whole team on board, it will serve as an excellent pretest if you are slated to present your recommendations to higher management.

Who's Really Responsible?

Don't let all the delegation and participation recommended above fool anyone; it's the *manager* who carries ultimate responsibility for every major choice of alternatives within his operation, no matter how that choice is actually made. The purpose of involving others in the evaluation process is *not to dilute* this responsibility. On the contrary, it is *to strengthen* it by putting the manager in the strongest possible position once the choice has been made. Having used the process and team procedures recommended here, he will have every right to expect the utmost cooperation once a decision has been made. Any action he might have to take (disciplinary or otherwise) to guarantee full support of the decision is more likely to be understood and backed up by all of the others who will have participated.

How to Spot a Poorly Made Decision

As a manager, you not only have to direct choices between alternatives, you also have to review decisions that *others* have managed. In some cases, you will have just as much to lose, if your review is superficial, as you would by having managed a poor decision yourself. In order to protect yourself and the organization that depends upon you, focus your questions on the *methods* and *approach* used by the decision makers, rather than the specific content of their recommendation. The reasoning here is that those who have developed the recommendation are sure to be more familiar with detail than anyone conducting a review. However, your very detachment as a reviewer makes you an excellent judge of *process,* which is the key to reliable decision making and the one thing people are likely to lose sight of in their struggle with masses of detail.

Here are some questions that can be very revealing of the extent to which others' thinking in evaluating alternatives followed an orderly process:

"What was the *problem* that triggered this study and recommendation?" (Listen to see if they began by identifying a specific deviation from plan. Was it clearly a *high-priority deviation?* If there is any doubt about the seriousness of the original problem, question them on *what criteria* were used in setting priorities. You may even want to push them to justify the use of these particular criteria as opposed to others that might have been applied.)

"What were the *probable causes* of this problem?" (Have they pinned down causation? How was their theory verified? What *other* possible causes were considered? Was an actual test run, and under what conditions?)

"What *other alternatives* were considered in coming to this recommendation?" (How many did they consider? How were these alternatives developed? Were they really serious about these other possibilities? What *good* features can they now see in the rejected alternatives?)

"*How* was the decision made?" (Did they apply a systematic approach? What criteria or decision factors were used? Where did these factors come from? Were they specified or classified in any way? Were they prioritized, and if so, on what basis? How were all these judgments combined to reach a decision?)

"What *weaknesses* do you see in the alternative you are recommending?" (If they see only few and minor ones, watch out! Was a serious potential problem analysis conducted? *Who* did it, the same people who favored the winning alternative? *How* were the potential problems integrated into the decision?)

"At what point in your analysis did you come to regard the alternative you are recommending as the best?" (Watch closely: did they have their minds made up early in the game and then devote most of their effort to documenting a preference based primarily on a hunch or on some personal motives?)

Your respondents will find these questions penetrating, and embarrassing if they haven't done their homework. Many people can fabricate impressive arguments for a favorite alternative, when pressed, but it's almost impossible to construct a whole decision-making process on the spur of the moment—particularly when the reviewer indicates he's interested in looking over the work sheets!

IN SUMMARY

This chapter on evaluating alternatives opened with a discussion of certain conditions that can blur effective decision making and then plunged into a brief but basic analysis of psychological forces in certain choice situations. Turning to practical managerial decision making, two approaches for evaluating alternatives were discussed. The favored one, decision analysis, was presented in some procedural detail, including recommendations on how to utilize others in a team approach that strengthens the decision but does not dilute any of the manager's authority.

chapter 7

Planning, Organizing, Controlling

THERE YOU ARE: 102 years old and stretched out on the beach watching your last sunset. You used to dread this moment; but since you dropped your favorite sport two years ago, life has hardly been worth living. A gentle numbness has taken over, and in these last moments your entire energy is concentrated on looking back over a long and eventful life.

What Do You See?

■ A succession of continuing efforts focused on goals that were important to you at successive stages in your life?

■ Or a series of unplanned responses to situations that came up and pressures that others brought to bear upon you?

When that time comes, it'll be too late to do anything but feel good or bad about what you've done. Now, fortunately, you can still alter the balance in your life between action and reaction. The process is called "planning": *the coordination of resources for scheduled goal achievement within anticipated environmental conditions.*

1. PLANNING

Planning in personal affairs is as old as history. Systematic, *long-range* planning in business is a relatively recent development. There are many executives who still feel it's a waste of time and effort. No one, they argue, knows enough about the future to be able to make reliable predictions of what will happen more than a short time ahead. Therefore, they feel the safest approach is *not* to get locked in on a single plan but to remain as flexible as possible in readiness to adapt to whatever comes up.

No one disputes the desirability of flexibility. The problem is *flexibility costs money.* Maintaining a state of readiness for multiple options requires resources in reserve, some of which won't be used once the direction of events becomes clear.

If Jack Stringer wants to "stay loose" so he could move on mini-boards, collapsible boards, jet boards, or whatever unexpected development surfers will swing for, he'll have to have designing capability, manufacturing versatility, manpower adaptability, training resources, *and available money.* He'll also have to be ready to phase out present production procedures, materials inventories, packaging, and maybe even Old Hans, on short notice.

Thus we see that while long-range planning involves costs of additional technical staff and a lot of time for communication and coordination between operations, the pressures of competition also force significant expenditures on an organization that just tries to keep its options open. In view of the limitations of prediction, probably the best approach is to strike a balance that involves *both* ideas:

1. Attempt to anticipate major trends in the environment and turn them to profit.

2. Maintain enough flexibility to change course in response to unexpected developments.

Proponents of long-range planning rightly point out that there are many things about the future we *can* anticipate with a high degree of certainty. For example, there isn't much doubt about the prediction that if you don't plant by 1970, you won't have a grove of ten-year-old trees in 1980. Obvious as this is, there are endless cases where this kind of predictive certainty has been overlooked, with subsequent regret. Uncontrolled stripping of natural resources, air and water pollution, missed investment opportunities, or just the failure to save are cases in point.

The Long and Short of It

The time span covered by long-range plans varies greatly. If you're in a business where it takes two to four years to develop a new product and the costs can break the whole enterprise if the new model is a failure, long-range plans probably should reach out seven years or more. On the other hand, a seven-year plan would be a farce in the ladies' garment industry: by that time the largest article of clothing may consist of a coyly carried purse.

Type of business, top-management attitude, financial resources, and organizational level are some of the variables that determine length of time covered by plans. Assuming he has long-term growth objectives, the president of Stoked Sports will have his staff studying population trends, projecting shifts in leisure time, and gathering data on spectator versus partici-patory sports activity with increasing standard of living. Time units under ten years won't mean much for questions like these.

Down in Jack Stringer's production department, the rele-vant environmental factors are rising costs of materials, recent union activity, seasonal supply of labor, and annual or semian-nual budget performance reviews. One year is the longest time span covered in Jack's plans.

Who Wants to Plan?

Another factor that affects many managers' outlook on plan-ning is their performance in the immediate past. Since mean-ingful planning takes time and effort, people whose operations have been highly successful without extensive planning usually resist the idea of investing in systematic, long-range planning. The suggestion that they might have done even bet-ter than they did, or that past success is no proof against fu-ture failure, often lands on deaf ears.

The man in trouble is likely to be much more receptive, provided he can see his way clear of the immediate crisis. His own hindsight tells him some of his difficulties could have been avoided with a little more forethought. Furthermore, if his predicament is forcing him to seek additional resources, he knows that the bankers will insist on seeing a well-developed plan.

Planning Misconceptions

Some of the controversy over the value of long-range planning is due to confusion over the purpose and process of planning. Let's try to clear up some of these points.

1. *Planning is not the prediction of future events.* It is only *today's* anticipations of what is most *likely* to occur. There's

quite a difference: the erroneous view (of planner as predictor) invites operating people to cast *their* plans in concrete and make minimum allowance for the unexpected, while the realization that all planning is largely an educated guessing game encourages preparation for contingencies. It also puts pressure on the planners to identify alternatives and estimate the probabilities of the various possibilities. Plans that reflect this kind of analysis are a much more valid representation of the inevitable limitations of the process.

2. *Planning is not the determination of future actions.* The main purpose of planning is to help make the best possible decision about what to do *right now*. No matter how far ahead we look in our efforts to anticipate probable developments, the real reason for doing so is to help us decide what is the best thing to do in the *immediate* future. In fact, one of the best ways to judge whether more extensive planning is advisable is to ask this question: "If we *knew* what will happen at that point, would it alter our decision about what to do *now?*"

3. *Planning should be a continuous activity, not a periodic one.* Ask most managers in large organizations for their strategic plan and they'll reach for it without a moment's hesitation, and you'll get dust on your hands as you start to look through it. It's not surprising that once the drudgery of grinding out a two-year, five-year, or whatever-year plan reaches the stage where a printed document exists, there is a general tendency to stick it up on the top shelf with the feeling that an unwelcome interruption is over and now we can get back to work!

One cause of this costly attitude toward long-range plans is an inappropriate planning cycle. If top management insists on detailed ten-year plans in a business where projections beyond a few months have proven unreliable, people will continue to regard long-range planning as an academic exercise until the planning cycle is shortened or greater insight into the factors affecting the business is gained.

Or it may be the planner's attitude that's at fault. Anyone who doesn't understand planning as a *continuous, dynamic process in which projections help guide actions whose results feed back revisions into the projections* is very likely to see plans as things that are written, followed, and only updated shortly before their time period has elapsed.

The Planning Process

Defined goals and alternative approaches to them will amount to little without detailed plans. A good plan helps an organization to:

- Translate broad goals into specific, measurable objectives
- Establish priorities between different activities
- Identify what must be done in order to obtain the desired results
- Allocate human and material resources
- Specify *when* each activity must occur
- Evaluate progress against schedule check-points

A plan is basically a schedule of activities. The manner in which it is developed makes a tremendous difference in its effectiveness. Two critical factors to be considered in designing a plan are *time perspective* and *roles of people*.

Clockwise versus Counterclockwise Planning

One way to draw up a plan is to begin by identifying the first thing that has to be done in order to get moving toward stated goals, estimate how long it will take to complete this first step, note the step 1 completion date, and then move on to step 2. If all the activity steps needed to reach the goals appear to be doable within a satisfactory time period, then the plan is considered ready for implementation. I call this "clockwise" planning in the sense that it takes the present as a starting point and moves *forward* toward the completion date.

"Counterclockwise" planning works *backward,* from completion date to the present. For example, if Jack Stringer plans to double his shaping productivity by November 1 through mechanization, his thinking might go something like this:

> Let's see, there's bound to be start-up problems with new equipment, so I better allow two weeks' "learning time" before we can expect to hit full production on a regular basis. This means we'll have to have the new equipment installed and more raw material rolling in by the middle of October.
>
> In order to install the new shaping machine, we're going to have to reinforce the floor. It will take two days to install the machine, and a week to rebuild the floor. The electricians have a couple of days' work that can't start until after the carpenters are out, so I better not start the alterations later than October 1. Even that doesn't allow for any foul-ups! I'd better get those carpenters in here not later than September 25, which was yesterday!

Sometimes the counterclockwise planner finds himself backed right up to the present with things still left to do. When that happens, there are three alternatives: delay completion dates, modify plans, or call in more resources. This may be unpleasant, but at least the problem is visible at a time when something can still be done about it.

Clockwise planning can also reveal unrealistic targets, but experience has shown the counterclockwise approach more likely to do so. Focusing on *end results and exactly what's needed to get them* seems to generate a more concrete view of time, money, and other resource requirements that will be needed. This is probably because the counterclockwise approach has a way of making the distant future look more like the present.

Who Gets into the Act?

When the plan in question deals with goals of an entire business and environmental factors likely to impact them, top-level executives and their staff will be the parties involved. Moving down from these overall "strategic" concerns to the operating level, the spectrum of people who can contribute effectively becomes much broader. In planning, just as in goal setting, we find that meaningful participation in the process not only makes for a better end product, but has significant motivational by-products.

Just what is likely to constitute "meaningful" participation in operational planning can be determined by considering *who* is likely to be affected by the plan. When it's a question of setting up a realistic schedule for mechanizing the shaping operation at Stoked, for example, Jack Stringer would certainly want to get Old Hans involved. Old Hans knows more about that operation than anyone else in the department, which means he's probably the most competent individual to estimate time and space requirements, and to anticipate possible problems. Furthermore, if Old Hans has any reservations about the changeover, his participation in planning it will certainly bring them to light. It is also the best known way to make a supporter of the new approach out of an actual or potential source of resistance.

While Jack must hold onto his authority for final approval of the changeover plans, the more detail of design he can delegate to subordinates, the better. The same holds for coordination between units; it's Jack's responsibility, but the more he can get Old Hans and whoever is in charge of raw materials inventory to work out the quantities and placement of materials among themselves and just fill Jack in on what they've decided, the better. Planning is like any other phase of the management process; its only purpose should be to help get work done more effectively (*not* to reaffirm organizational authority). Therefore, the more of a role the individual who will actually do the work has in it, the more likely it is that the plans will be realistic, understood, and supported.

2. ORGANIZING

The purpose of organizing is to establish formal *and informal* relationships among people and activities that most efficiently implement plans. These relationships of people and activities can be defined in great detail or sketched in general outlines that leave room for exploration and variation. Organization structures are sometimes maintained in essentially the same form for long periods of time; in other cases they are continually changing. The degree of detail in organization design and the constancy of structure over time vary widely depending upon the kind of business, environmental factors, attitudes of top management, skills of employees, and a host of other variables. In fact, there are so many unknowns in this area that no one's authoritative knowledge extends very far beyond what he has actually experienced, and even then he may be quite misled about the underlying causes of what he has seen and felt.[24]

For example, a manager who has spent his days in a tightly structured, closely controlled, and highly successful organization is almost sure to recommend detailed job descriptions, specific objectives, and spelled-out measures of work accomplished. Yet his own subordinates might tell you that they got their work done *in spite of*, rather than *because of*, "all the nit-picking around there!"

By contrast, there's the easygoing manager who prides himself on treating his people like "professionals" and thereby getting high-quality work. He may never know how much *more* high-quality work would result if his people had a clearer idea of work priorities and of who is responsible for what in his department. As it is, lots of time gets lost in "jurisdictional disputes" over responsibilities, and deadlines are sometimes missed because parts of the job "fell between the chairs."

How Much Structure?

Every manager will have to feel his way toward the balance between defined limits and freedom that is appropriate for his type of work, number of people, and kind of people. In general, severe time pressures, large numbers of people, inexperience, and low skill level require sharper delineation of authority, responsibility, and specific job description. But even this generalization must be qualified because the definition of boundaries does *not* necessarily limit freedom and creativity. On the contrary: *a clearly defined work boundary can help release creative capacity by clearly marking out the territory within which innovation is needed* and giving an individual the understanding that this is *his* field of opportunity.

Probably the best safeguard for striking a balance on structure is to make frequent checks on how your people react to the current form and degree of compartmentalization in your organization. Watch for:

- Confusion over responsibilities
- Jealousy over authority
- Jobs that get done twice
- Work left undone
- Lack of cooperation
- Communication breakdowns
- Excessive demands upon *your* time

These symptoms have a variety of possible causes, one of which is *either* too tight or too loose an organization structure.

Need for Consistency

It is very easy to inadvertently organize people and work so conflict is certain to arise. The way in which staff personnel are used by one of the country's largest businesses offers an excellent example.

This company, like many, has a series of functional staffs like marketing, manufacturing, engineering, research, finance, and legal that have been established as services to line management. These staff units are responsible for keeping abreast of the latest developments in their respective functional areas and for assisting their line counterparts in any way they can. However, these same staffs are also required to submit a monthly report to the president on all problems encountered.

The purpose of these problem reports by staff is simply to give top management a more complete picture of the company's state of health. The effect, however, is to make many line managers leery of staff. When a staff man shows up on a line operation, the reaction of many is, "Is he here to help, or to spy?"

The lesson I derive from this case is that in designing organization units and relationships between units, one should be very clear on the fundamental purpose of each particular unit and relationship. If more than one purpose is to be served, be sure they are truly compatible.

Organizations Must Be Dynamic

The rate of change in most competitive businesses today is accelerating. Since organization is the set of relationships established to perform the work of a business, it must also be capable of change. This is more complicated than it sounds. What t really means is that *a good organization structure includes the means of sensing the need for change and for redesigning itself.*

This is not typical of most organizations. On the contrary, once an organization structure is established there are many forces that tend to keep its structure static. Here are some of the stronger ones:

■ People at or near the top want to keep the power they have.

■ People who are climbing want to keep the structure they have learned to climb.

■ Even people at the bottom want to keep the structure they have learned to survive.

■ Change requires extra effort.

With forces like these operating, organizations are certain to fall behind the needs of the business unless self-evaluation and change has been built into the structure. This can be done by having a particular unit such as an "organization renewal staff" assigned the responsibility of recommending continual improvements, but it's much better to get *everyone* in on the act. To accomplish this, each organization unit should be charged with periodically reviewing the appropriateness of its own size, location in the system, communication channels, dependencies, etc. Involving all units in the development of recommendations for organizational change does not eliminate the need for the organization renewal staff. They still have the important functions of:

(1) making sure people's desire to preserve the status quo doesn't overpower their desire for improvement

(2) taking the company-wide overview that is necessary for effective integration of the unit-by-unit recommendations

How often should organization structure be reviewed? There has been lots of controversy over this question, with many observers feeling that reorganizations are costly in terms of time required for relearning and upsetting to people's morale. I have personally experienced departmental reorganizations where everyone "held their breath" for about six months: three waiting to see what would happen to whom, and three carefully feeling out what is and is not acceptable under the new administration. From such experiences, one could conclude that reorganizations should be as few and far between as possible.

Note, however, that all these problems are related to the fact that this reorganization was something that was done *to* the people in the department. When the changes involve a significant contribution *by* the people themselves, it is quite a different situation.

- It comes as no surprise.
- Many actually look forward to it.
- They will have started to think about their new responsibilities before the changeover, enabling rapid adjustment to new roles.

Under these circumstances, organization change can be responsive to market shifts, new technology, competitive factors, and other external forces. Organizations quick to *sense* change have often been beat out by others who were slower to perceive, but quicker to react in a productive manner.

Organization Design to People or to Work?

Which makes the most sense?

1. To design an organization structure strictly from the point of view of the *work to be done,* beginning with a well-defined picture of the total work needed and breaking this down into units that can be performed by departments and ultimately individual people?

2. To design from the point of view of the *individuals available and the skills they possess,* letting the human factor be the primary determinant of the number, size, and relationship of work units that make up the organization?

While the total work to be accomplished must be the starting point for organization design, the definition of work subunits and relationships between subunits without regard to the particular individuals that will be performing the work is impractical and unrealistic. Just the same, it has been the standard approach to job design.

This attempt to force people into preconceived units of work and preconceived relationships is a major cause of the widely observed discrepancies between "formal" and "informal" organization structure. Preferring not to be programmed, people forget or reject their job descriptions and proceed to do the work in their own way and establish relationships among each other that weren't designed into the organization chart.

One result of this has been hundreds of man-years of work for social scientists, who have gloried in their findings of discrepancies between the formal organization charts and what people were actually doing down on the plant floor and in the offices. Another more costly result has been the tremendous loss of managerial control plus the tension and friction generated by conflict between "what management prescribed" and "what really seems to work around here."

Therefore, when designing organizations and reorganizations, it pays to think about who, specifically, will be doing each piece of work. Best of all, the individual himself should be consulted, and invited to continue his inputs as he gathers experience in the new position. This takes more time than trying to issue a master plan complete down to the position descriptions, but it has a lot more chance of producing a viable organization structure.

Practically, the only way to create such a "living design" for an entire organization is to have the discussions occurring at each managerial level, involving each manager and his subordinates, on a recurring basis. It actually becomes part of the participative planning process, and the recommendations from all sources should be integrated and finalized right along with unit work objectives.

Building Blocks of Organization

Participation in goal setting, alternative development, decision making, planning, and reorganization goes a long way toward motivating people. Whether the good intentions ever get translated into useful activity depends a lot on how the work to be done is actually divided up among the individuals and groups who are supposed to do it. Here are some suggestions:

1. The work of an organization unit should be divided into "man-sized" portions, so that each individual can get a sense of real accomplishment for himself and contribution to the group.

2. While these pieces of work must be doable, they should also be sufficiently difficult for the individual to feel challenged as he approaches the work and to have a sense of achievement when he completes it.

3. The units of work must be measurable, and standards must be established (if achievement is to be felt). The measures and standards should be understood and applicable by both the individual and his manager.

4. All work should be structured to permit a balance of individual work and teamwork. People need both: individual achievement and a share in group activity.

5. Have each individual spend as much of his time as possible doing work that he alone can do. Utilization of unique capabilities is a great self-motivator.

These aren't easy prescriptions to fill, since there are other factors like materials, machines, and product design that limit the ways in which work can be structured. Here is another situation where participation by those who will actually perform the work can work wonders. The five points on organizing work won't be perfectly implemented, but their sharing in the attempt usually creates a greater tolerance for shortcomings, and will probably produce a better fit between individual and work.

How to Promote

The continuing success of an organization structure probably depends more on promotion practice than any other single variable. Since personnel are always changing, it is promotion that mostly determines who is doing what with whom in the long run. Even more important, promotions are the thing people look to as the real proof of what kind of behavior "pays off" in their organization. If promotions consistently go to the individual who spends the most time in the boss's office, then "sticking close to the boss" will be regarded as the way to get ahead, regardless of what top management says and writes about the matter.

The most frequently used criteria for promotion are not the best, in my opinion. They center around the judgment of an individual's *potential* for the higher-level job. A set of characteristics judged to be important for effective performance of the job are identified, and candidates are compared for their possession of these characteristics. Typical characteristics for managerial positions are aggressiveness, leadership ability, analytical ability, communications skills, physical image, etc. This promotion procedure involves two critical and questionable steps:

1. Identification of the personal characteristics that make for managerial success

2. Evaluation of candidates' possession, or probable development of these characteristics

A contrasting and much simpler approach has been used by some executives with great success. It uses a single criterion for promotion: *performance* on present job. The position taken here is that regardless of his "image," background, or apparent communication skills, the individual who has been the top producer on the job should get the first chance at the higher position.

I consider this a very sound approach because:

■ This individual has already demonstrated strong motivation, which I believe to be the number one requirement for successful managing.

■ The selection is based on an objective, measurable, and highly visible criterion.

- Knowledge of the work will help him keep things under control while he's learning more about managing.
- He is more likely to have others' respect than any other individual in the operation.
- When others see that the best performer gets first crack at the top job, it will have a very positive effect on *their* work motivation.

An outstanding example of successful application of promotion by performance is IBM's office products manufacturing plant in Lexington, Kentucky. Mr. Clair Vough, IBM vice-president and general manager who rose from the ranks, has built his entire management philosophy around the pay and promote for performance concept. The result has been high productivity, high morale, and profitability.

Fitting Managers to Work

"A good manager can manage anything!"

"Put a personnel manager in charge of Engineering and he'll fall flat on his fat 'you-know-what'! You've got to know how to *do* the work if you're going to *manage* it."

Here's another critical organization issue that has caused plenty of fur to fly. Some companies, like General Electric, have made a practice of shifting managers from function to function, as part of a planned program to develop good general managers. The price that may have been paid at the functional level has never been measured.

Managing, as these chapters hopefully demonstrate, involves a set of principles and skills that apply in a wide variety of organizations, at all levels of management, and to people involved in very different kinds of work. However, familiarity with the work *content* of the positions he supervises is a great help to a manager's ability to understand his subordinates' needs and gain their respect. It also helps him tremendously in hiring, training, and evaluating performance.

3. CONTROLLING

Control means keeping things on track. The first step is to have a good, clear track, which is why we opened this chapter with a discussion of planning. Next, one needs a smooth-running, well-coordinated machine, which is why we went into some principles of organization. But even the best equipment, following well-established procedures, will run into unforeseen difficulties from time to time.

Some of these deviations from plan can be anticipated and avoided. Some can be detected by an early warning system in time to reduce the seriousness of their impact. Some can't be helped. A method for identifying potential problems that were not considered in the original plans will be presented later in this section. Right now, let's take a critical look at the general process for tracking and evaluating performance. To do this, we need standards. In my opinion a good tracking system should be:

■ *Sensitive* so it gives early warnings rather than just disaster reports

■ *Analytical* of observed deviations from plan in order to pinpoint underlying causes wherever possible

■ *Diplomatic* in its early focus on *situations* rather than *individuals* as causes of deviations from plan

■ *Corrective* in the sense that wherever a quick and feasible fix is available the control point won't hesitate to put it into effect

■ *Economical* in its minimization of additional personnel and superimposed organization structures

Two Contrasting Approaches

Most organizations separate major parts of the control function from other work elements such as sales and production.

Typically, much of the most important control work is put in the hands of financial people for two reasons:

1. Deviations from plan inevitably produce financial consequences (which are the ultimate concern of the business).

2. Financial people have been trained in a discipline that stresses objectivity and has some excellent methods for measuring a wide range of activity.

The control function of finance is reflected in organizational relationships. Even though the formal organization chart usually shows finance as one of several functions reporting to a general manager, all financial people in a company belong to a tightly knit, informal group often referred to as the "financial fraternity." Special allegiance and private communication channels are maintained as means of getting vital information from the point of observation to the top of the organization as quickly as possible and with as little distortion as possible.

Other staffs, such as Manufacturing and Personnel, are also used for purposes of control. This practice of putting primary responsibility for control in the hands of special groups (which I call a "centralized" approach to control) has two major shortcomings:

1. The people whose work is under surveillance tend to feel less responsible for maintaining their own control.

2. A lack of trust sometimes develops between the controlling and the controlled groups.

These are important considerations. Not infrequently they combine to produce an attitude of trying to beat the system instead of supporting it. A prime example is the widespread falsification of expense accounts and the cavalier attitude that goes with it.

A contrasting and much rarer approach to control places primary responsibility for noting, reporting, and correcting deviations from plan in the hands of the individuals who actually do the work. No special communication channels are established: all problem reports must come up through the regular line management organization.

This "decentralized" approach to control deprives top management of a private set of "eyes," but the trust it implies can have some powerful motivational payoffs in the form of conscientious *self-control*. It is pretty well established psychologically that trust begets trust, while distrust begets distrust.

A striking example of high trust is the case of a West Coast corporation that adopted the practice of sending signed, blank checks to all suppliers right along with the order, leaving the supplier free to fill in whatever dollar amount he chose. They experienced no cheating, large savings from reduced clerical work, and credit for early payment.

I contrast these two extremes in order to emphasize a point. *Control, whose very purpose is to reduce risk, inevitably involves taking risk.* One either risks costly procedures and low trust, or less and later information about problems. No one has figured out a way to win on both counts, though many have inadvertently lost on both.

Controlling Misconceptions

Here are two prevalent ideas about control that have caused lots of unnecessary friction and frustration:

1. Organizational control inevitably runs counter to the individual human's desire for freedom; stripped of euphemisms, it amounts to a modified form of dictatorship.

This view results from looking at only one aspect of control, the limitation it involves. This element is necessary whenever and wherever people live and work together, simply because some of man's instinctive drives have destructive consequences for other men when left uninhibited.

However, in a world where few live alone, control is also an essential instrument of freedom. It defines for individuals and groups the areas in which *they* have authority, and where *they* can exercise their creative capacities with minimum conflict. A recent study within one of the country's largest and most successful organizations revealed that many middle managers wanted a *clearer definition of authority and more distinction made between departmental missions* by top management. In a sense, they were asking for *more* control in order to have a freer hand *within* their area of responsibility.

2. Top management's problem is to strike the balance between too much and too little control.

This statement is an oversimplification. It can, and has led to well-meant but fruitless management reactions to internal assessments of "overcontrol" or "undercontrol." When morale is sagging and attrition increasing because people feel overaudited and under excessive surveillance, a swing toward the other pole does not necessarily solve the problem. The reason: *lack* of structure can be just as limiting as overstructure. This has been established experimentally and used as a deliberate device to keep people off balance.

Conversely, when costs soar and unanticipated problems crop up all over the place, "clamping down the lid" through tighter monitoring of activities can make things even worse. It may very well be that the problems were caused by confusion over objectives; such confusion is unlikely to be cleared up just by closer supervision. If anything, resentment will be added to the confusion.

Both of these overreactions are due to lack of precision in diagnosing the problem. The study referred to above showed that criticism of top-management "control" can actually mean the following specific conditions existing *all at the same time:*

1. Too frequent and too detailed audits
2. Inadequate measures of performance
3. Unclear missions and goals
4. Ambiguous delegation of authority
5. Overly detailed specification of corporate prerogatives

The conclusion I draw is that *good control requires mutually understood and acceptable definitions of both limitations and freedoms.* These definitions must be *specific enough so both parties feel they know what's expected of them, but not so detailed that they imply lack of trust or prohibit the use of judgment in their application.*

Consistency Again

The approach to control that you select cannot make a success of your entire management method, but it can break it. If you have invited participation in defining goals, identifying alternatives, choosing between alternatives, planning, and organizing, and then if you proceed to monitor people's performance on a day-to-day basis through a special security force, don't expect them to take your words about teamwork very seriously. They know that *your approach to control is the real telltale on how much trust you put in their attitude and ability.*

Thus when it comes to control, we quote the old circus barker, backwards, "You takes your choice, and you pays your money!" I believe that high trust will be low cost in this case.

Anticipating Problems

Trusting people doesn't mean simply turning them loose. You can help your subordinates in their self-control by providing them with tools to more effectively prevent and correct problems on their own. The entire next chapter will deal with a detailed method of diagnosing and correcting problems that have already occurred. Right now, let's take a look at some methods for reducing the likelihood that serious problems ever take place.

Potential problem analysis, another area in which Kepner-Tregoe Associates have done extensive work, is an educated guessing game. It is based on the assumption that resources for control are always limited, and therefore a method of allocating these resources that takes advantage of past experience and logical judgment will be more efficient than trying to watch and prepare for every possible failure (which is impossible) or just barging ahead with the hope that nothing serious will go wrong (which is unlikely). Specifically, this process consists of a set of guides for setting priorities on things that might go wrong. These priorities, in turn, help direct the decisions as to:

- Where and when special surveillance is advisable
- Who should be alerted if trouble does develop
- What kinds of backup resources should be on hand
- Where alternative procedures should be identified
- How plans need to be modified right now

Stepwise Process

The following steps are in necessary sequence. Skipping steps or taking them out of order will almost certainly reduce their reliability.

1. *What could go wrong?* Plans in hand, this is the first question to ask. Ideally, it should be aimed at each stage of the plan by the people who will be responsible for implementation (preferably *not* the original planners). Like early stages in goal setting and creating alternatives, this should be done in a freewheeling, brainstorming atmosphere. Don't reject any suggestions at this point, for fear of inhibiting imagination. As in creating alternatives, evaluation is a separate phase.

2. *Set priorities.* It would be impossible and wasteful to try to prepare for or prevent all the potential problems a motivated group can dream up. In order to cut the list down to manageable size and still preserve essential items, each suggestion should be evaluated against these criteria:

   a. *Seriousness* (harm done if it *does* happen)
   b. *Probability* (how *likely* it is to happen)

These two judgments should be made independently of each other, to protect against the halo effect of a very serious potential problem looming so large that people lose sight of the fact that it is extremely unlikely.

3. *Establish preventive or corrective action.* All items judged to be both serious and likely should now be examined to see what particular form of surveillance, backup, or replanning will produce adequate protection at a reasonable cost. If the price of protection seems high, there are further analytical steps that can focus controls more sharply and reduce costs.

4. *Identify possible causes.* For each potential problem where control is difficult or costly, invite the people who are most familiar with that particular type of operation to list all the conditions they can think of that might trigger the problem. Again, this should be a creative, not an evaluative activity, so hold off any criticism of the causal suggestions until the next step.

5. *Prioritize possible causes.* The field must be narrowed once more. This time there is no question about seriousness, since only potentially serious problems were considered. There are two kinds of probability to be rated, however:

a. *Probability of occurrence* (how likely the condition that might cause the problem is to even take place)

b. *Probability to cause* (how likely the condition, if it *does* happen, is to actually cause the problem)

Just reading in the abstract, this may sound like we're slicing pretty thin on something that's only guesswork anyway. Actually, this kind of organized anticipation has paid off heavily in a wide variety of situations. If you want to test it, just consider some of the costly accidents and failures you've witnessed. In many cases even just a little extra forethought could have saved money, embarrassment, even lives.

Generators that powered the pumps in the sinking *Andrea Doria* were put out of commission by water flowing in through a tunnel in the deep fuel tank compartment that bypassed the bulkheads. The cabin air intake of a passenger plane sucked in fuel that was being jettisoned and blew up the aircraft. A supersecret, unmanned antisubmarine helicopter went out of control on its test flight and disappeared in the vicinity of Russian trawlers! The first of a fleet of special maintenance trucks for the Holland Tunnel struck the top of the tunnel entrance on its first run. The mayor of Philadelphia, commemorating the city's new mechanized and superefficient post office, had difficulty mailing the first letter: there wasn't a letter drop!

The preventive steps in each of these cases would have been simple and inexpensive. No one is perfect, but it's hard to believe that some systematic anticipation wouldn't have pinpointed the possibility of some of these catastrophies, particularly if people who *didn't* draw up the plans had been involved. This team approach to control design also has the advantage of avoiding a lot of "I could have told you so" expressions. Being in on the attempt to anticipate problems leaves one with a big stake in the plan's success.

IN SUMMARY

This chapter has dealt with three closely related phases of managerial work: planning, organizing, and controlling. Processes, pitfalls, and opportunities for involving employees were discussed for each phase. Resistance to planning, the time dimension in planning, formal and informal organization, tight versus loose organization structuring, the need for continual reorganization, contrasting approaches to control, and potential problem analysis were the major issues covered.

chapter 8

Analyzing Deviations

No matter how thorough the planning, how orderly the organizing, and how careful the control, there will almost always be deviations from plan: problems! That's why, among other things, every manager is a professional problem solver. Just to keep your job as a manager requires a reasonably favorable balance of problems solved to problems created or left unsolved. As a matter of fact, a certain minimum balance of this kind is required just to stay alive.

Consciously and unconsciously, every human being devotes a major portion of his mental energy to problem solving, beginning long before he could walk or talk. Each individual develops a highly personal style of tackling problems that becomes so deeply engrained it operates on a completely automatic basis. It never even occurs to most people that there might be value in examining the *method* they use in solving problems, any more than it would occur to them to question how they walk.

Even managers, whose very livelihood depends heavily upon their problem-solving skill, typically limit their reviews to the *results* of problem-solving activity instead of studying the *process* that was applied. Of thousands I have observed, less than one in twenty managers ever took the trouble, on their own, to examine and evaluate their approach to solving problems. Many resist the process even when encouraged to study it on company time.

Sources of Resistance

There are a number of factors that work against systematic self-analysis of problem-solving technique, even though we readily proclaim how much *others* would benefit from this kind of exercise.

1. *Rewards for results.* Higher managers rarely inquire into details of process. They simply want to know the results, good or bad, and they reward or penalize pretty much on that basis. Some even take the position that inquiry into methods runs counter to proper practice of delegation.

2. *Time pressures.* Self-analysis of system does take time, and the time to do it in depth is not in the heat of deadline pressures. Particularly in the early stages, this kind of investigation and evaluation should be undertaken in a quiet, relaxed atmosphere where a course of events and decisions can be examined and reexamined from several points of view.

3. *Fear of failure.* If you're a manager, you're already a winner compared to the vast majority who will never obtain the authority and responsibility you already bear. Under these circumstances, it's quite natural to be anxious about tampering

with anything so basic as your problem-solving technique. There's always the concern that once you take a skill like this apart, it may be very difficult to put it together again.

4. *Force of habit.* Most of us have experienced the difficulty involved in changing strong habits. It takes a tremendous effort of self-discipline, and even then we frequently relapse into our old accustomed ways. Many people instinctively sense that changing a habit of thought process will be one of the most difficult things they ever tried, and they're right.

But there are compensations for the daring and energetic. For one thing, any serious effort at self-analysis of the problem-solving technique is certain to identify strengths to retain and weaknesses to eliminate. Furthermore, improvement in problem solving isn't a matter of struggling from misery to mastery. The impact of this managerial activity is so widespread that even a slight improvement, *consistently applied,* is sure to produce results and be noticed.

Different Approaches

For comparison's sake and because different methods of problem analysis fit different individual styles of thinking, let's look briefly at some distinguishable approaches to deviation analysis:

"Pure Intuitive" This is my tag name for the approach that has no conscious awareness of any thought processes between the perception of a problem and proposals for corrective action. It's the most natural approach to problem solving and also the fastest. It is *not* the most reliable.

"Semi-intuitive" This modifies the pure intuitive approach in one important step: there is a conscious effort to identify the *cause* of a problem before going on to corrective action. While there is no conscious method for pinpointing causes, the break

in the intuitive leap from problem to action brings a great re-
duction in risk.

"Systematic" We're about to illustrate a particular example of
consciously controlled, step-by-step analysis that attempts to
make each stage in the thought process of problem solving visible to the individual or team involved. Though difficult, this
is believed to offer maximum control.

Getting Down to Cases

Concepts of problem solving are difficult to communicate
through lecture or written theory. Even though important,
they come through dry and unappetizing. Much more effective, and fun, is to tackle a case problem, see how you do, and
then see how the information would be handled in a step-by-
step systematic approach.

That's what we'll do here. Consider yourself a high-priced
consultant that has been called in by the Stoked Sports top
management to bail them out of the crisis described below.
Once you've taken a crack at the problem, we'll work it over
together so you can compare your approach to one I've found
useful.

The first inkling of the problem was a telegram:

> STOP SHIPMENT OF SPECIALS STOP RETURNING FIVE FOR REPAIR OR
> REPLACEMENT STOP MIAMI MAR SHOP

It was only the beginning! Wires and irate letters were also
coming in from California, their biggest market, in growing
numbers. The only region not to complain about the new
Stoked Special was the Northeast, and harried home office executives were expecting them with each mail delivery.

It was a honeymoon turned nightmare for Jack Stringer.
The Stoked Special had been his own creation, hailed by
Surflife as ". . . the greatest surfing breakthrough since the

introduction of the short board." More important, the special had been an instant sales success in all areas.

Jack's concept had been to develop a board that would satisfy (1) the novice, (2) the virtuoso, (3) the small-wave rider, (4) the big-wave rider, and (5) the traveling surfer, all in one vehicle. His product was a triple section board that could be assembled in a short or long form (by either omitting or including the middle section). Here's a sketch of the "5-in-1 Special" complete with lettering decor:

The two sections making up the "STUD" were formed of the lightest foam available. Each of these sections weighed 5 pounds, so that including the 8-ounce skeg, the 7-foot STUD weighed only 10½ pounds. In order to add the "body" as well as length needed for a big wave board, Jack had the "OK" section made of denser foam so that even though shorter, it weighed 6 pounds. A special 42- by 26-inch carrying case with handgrip and shoulder strap was designed in two styles: psychedelic color patterns for the young; simulated leather for the young at heart.

Technically, the only real challenge in the special was to make a joint that would permit easy assembly and yet be as strong as the rest of the board when assembled. This was accomplished with what Jack called his "double-notched, long-lap joint." In cross section, it looked like this:

The locking bolt and built-in socket were chromed and slotted so they could be tightened with a quarter. The notches ran the width of the board, so only a single bolt was needed to lock in each unit. The middle section could be ordered in a 2- or 3-foot length.

The Stoked Special hit the market in December, in time for Christmas. By April 1, with over a thousand sold, top management was considering a promotion for Stringer. Then, in June, came the bad news. Phone calls with Miami Mar and San Diego San and Sea netted the following complaints:

"When the surf's up, this thing is down!"

"Screw-holes won't line up for Long Form."

"Ends are okay, but the OK section won't fit."

Examination of eighteen returned specials confirmed the complaints: the end sections mated, but not with the midsection. This was a real puzzler, particularly since it was obvious that the midsections hadn't been used nearly as much as the ends on any of the returned boards.

Action Called For

What would you do if you were in Stringer's position:
- Reinforce the midsection against warping?
- Drop the big-wave option (omit midsections)?
- Use low-density foam throughout?
- Discontinue the special altogether?
- Apply for early retirement?

Only one of these alternatives might have helped, and even that one involves a significant sacrifice. But before considering conclusions, why don't you go ahead and analyze the problem. You have enough information about the situation to make some sound recommendations.

The approach I prefer has been developed over many years by logicians, military tacticians, educators, and management consultants. Some excellent refinements have been formalized by Kepner-Tregoe Associates and are described with examples in the first nine chapters of their book, *The Rational Manager*. If you find the following method helpful, I urge you to add to your understanding by reading in Kepner-Tregoe.

The primary purpose of the approach is to reduce chances of costly and ineffective action, with minimum delay for analysis. Essentially, the method organizes readily available information in a way that emphasizes:

- Facts, rather than theories
- Missing information
- Possible causes
- Probabilities of causes

It also offers a set of guidelines for *managing* a problem analysis when information is dispersed and several people have to be involved. We will go into this team aspect of deviation analysis after first illustrating a logic for dealing with the information.

Define the Deviation

Before plunging into detailed analysis of the problem at hand, it's a good idea to make sure it really warrants your first attention. Managers, after all, rarely face only *one* problem (unless they're about to be fired)! Therefore, if there's any question at all, a moment spent checking priorities will be time well spent. Call it insurance against a superior's snide comment, "Congratulations, Stringer, you've done a magnificent job on your No. 3 problem!"

Priorities are usually pretty clear in a business you know. About the only danger is to have one factor, like immediate costs, loom so large that it blots out other important considerations. To guard against this, compare the negative deviations you face for *each* of these priority criteria:

- *Cost* (actual or threatened loss of money)
- *Timing* (does delay really matter?)
- *Information* (enough on hand for preliminary analysis)

The purpose of this check is *not* to decide which deviation is your "worst" problem. It is to help decide which you should tackle *first* and to provide a rationale for this decision if it's ever challenged.

With a top-priority deviation selected, the first step in analysis is to organize the information on hand in a way that sharpens the limits of the problem. The categories of time, place, amount, item, and source help as a checklist to ensure that all useful information has been noted. Here's how the Stoked crisis could be sorted out:

	Reported	*Not reported*
ITEM:	New Stoked Specials Midsections won't fit Screw-holes don't line up	Other models End sections
SOURCE:	Surfers, dealers Our shop (checked returns)	Quality Control check
PLACE:	Florida Southern California	Northeast
TIME:	June and following (7 months after first sales)	Prior to June
AMOUNT:	18 returned 2 large dealers Increasing numbers	Actual number of complaints Any sign of leveling or of decrease

Certain ground rules should be kept in mind when a deviation is classified in this manner.

1. *Focus on only one problem.* The analysis will become confused if information about several problems gets combined. To prevent this, it's a good idea to *name* your problem before beginning to sort it out. Stringer could have named his: "Customer Complaints about Specials."

2. *List facts only.* This is not the time for opinions. What you want in this first information sort is just what is known about the item, source, place, time, and amount of your top-priority problem. Note that the Reported–Not Reported chart

is primarily a device for focusing attention on what is known and believable about the problem up to the moment, and contrasting this with items, places, times, etc., that have *not* yet produced reports of trouble.

In our case, the façt that no complaints have come in from the Northeast doesn't mean that some are on the way or that there never will be any from that region. All it means is that barring further information, it's more likely that the problem hasn't hit the Northeast than that it has.

3. *Avoid theories of cause.* This is the most difficult of all, since the very purpose of deviation analysis is to identify probable causes. Nevertheless, causal theories must be set aside at the definition stage or they will almost certainly short-circuit the entire analysis by drawing attention to just *some* of the facts.

When people give you theories instead of facts, you have a choice. If you believe they are correct, then drop any further analysis and get on with the identification of corrective alternatives. If you are in doubt, file their idea for future checking once all the readily available facts have been sorted out.

Look for Differences

The next step in deviation analysis is to compare each entry of Reported information with its Not Reported counterpart. Differences between them may contain leads to possible causes. For example, the Item Reported involves midsections, while end section trouble was Not Reported. Jack could list a number of differences between the midsection versus end sections:

- midsections are rectangular; end sections triangular.
- midsections are uniformly thick; end sections taper.
- midsections are made of different material (denser foam).
- midsections are heavier than end sections.
- midsections are used less than end sections.

Differences between Reported and Not Reported information about Source of complaints led Stringer to note trouble was reported only *after:*

- shipment to dealers
- handling and storage at dealers
- customer use and storage

Contrasting Place entries, Stringer noted that complaints to date were all from areas where:

- the climate was much warmer
- surfing was much better
- surfers were more experienced

Time entries didn't yield any additional differences, but they emphasize the difference in climate (spring) between the Northeast as opposed to Florida and Southern California. All the Amount information did was to make Jack worry even more: he obviously had an escalating problem on his hands. There wasn't any point in noting this, however, since it was already stated in the definition of the deviation.

There Must Be a Change

There never was a problem without a change. Don't ask me why. It's just the way the world was put together. Surfboard or satellite, if the thing was functioning satisfactorily at one point in time and then broke down at another, something obviously changed; and that something is part of what we call the "cause" of the problem. It isn't necessarily the *entire* cause, because there may have been *more than one change,* and there may have been some *other conditions* that contributed to the problem. These "other conditions" may be differences that always existed.

For example, suppose you and I had lunch together and ate some foul seafood that made me sick but didn't phase you. That could happen, because you probably have a less sensitive gastrointestinal tract than I do. Okay, so you're lucky. The point is, *What caused me to get sick?* The crucial change that took place between my being well and sick was eating the seafood. But if the seafood were the *sole* (no pun intended) cause of my sickness, why didn't you get sick too?

So we see that a problem can be caused by a change *and* a difference. Problems can be caused by *any number* of changes and differences, and this has important consequences for corrective action. Even though a problem has a causal pattern of three changes and five differences, counteracting only one change or one of the differences may be all it takes to correct the problem and prevent its recurrence. (Feed me good food and you'll never guess I have a sensitive digestive system.)

This logic might lead one to settle for a system of deviation analysis that comes up with only one cause. That could be costly. Even if the problem can be fixed with only one corrective action, different actions have very different costs. Therefore, a system that identifies as many of the major factors (changes *and* differences) as possible without unreasonable costs of analysis is the one we want. This way, you have more options for corrective alternatives.

Changes from Differences

Since things are always happening at Stoked Sports and everywhere else, Stringer won't have any difficulty finding one or more changes that might have caused complaints about his special. If he has any shortage of imagination, Old Hans and others in the shop are sure to be ready with theories. That's just the trouble: *changes* are so close to *causes* (every change *is* one possible cause) that once you invite suggestions, you're likely to be flooded.

The trick is to identify the changes that are most likely to be real causal factors in the problem. The way to do this is *see what changes are included in, or suggested by, the differences you found between where and when the problem occurred and didn't occur.*

In Stringer's case, all he has to do is look over the differences he has already listed and see which ones involve changes. Several come to mind:

■ temperature changes in use (from hot beach to cool water)

■ pressure changes (stresses in use)

■ torque changes (in use and storage)

Since the special can be used without the OK section but not without both the ST and UD sections, Stringer also knows that one of these or all these changes may have much more effect on the end sections than the midsection. He also knows that even in cases where all three sections were equally exposed, the difference in materials may have resulted in different reactions to the temperature and stress changes. This could also be true for the different shapes.

Changes and differences are the raw materials from which theories of probable causation are constructed. Personally, I think it is wiser to talk in terms of possible (rather than probable) causes at this point, just as an added precaution against accepting untested explanations. Here are some of the possible causes Stringer put together from his changes and differences:

1. With age, use, and exposure, any board warps to some extent. Different degrees of warping between the midsection and the end sections may be due to the difference in density of foam used in the midsection versus the end sections.

2. Heat is critical in warping. Surfers would use the STUD much more than the STOKUD everywhere, but the greater heat in Florida and California caused more warping in the end sections, leaving the middle a misfit (since the joined end sections would warp congruently).

3. The triangular and slightly conical shape of the two end sections could be more resistant to warping than the rectangular and relatively flat midsection. Therefore the midsection, stored unattached, might be more likely to warp due either to inherent materials stresses or to the weight of other articles left on top of it in storage.

Testing Possible Causes

When several possible causes have been found (and don't ever settle for just one unless it's an open-and-shut case), the next step is to decide which one is your best bet. One way to do this is to run some actual tests that compare the different theories and see which one helps most to eliminate the complaint. Jack Stringer could have some specials made using the same density foam throughout and send them out on test to New York and Miami in order to see if this eliminated or reduced his problem. He could also have half of his test specials used only in the STUD version, with the OK section carefully stored, while the other half of the sample would always be kept in the complete STOKUD form.

He would probably learn useful things from these tests, but the expense would be significant and Stoked's reputation might suffer in the field. Fortunately, there is a very quick and inexpensive way to run a first test on possible causes. This involves simply checking them back against the original definition of the problem to see if they hold up, logically.

Using Jack's first possible cause as an example, the way to test logically is to ask this question:

> *If* the sole cause of the complaints were warping due to the different materials used, *then* would we expect the complaints to -
>
> . . . be about specials and not other models? (Yes)
>
> . . . claim the midsections won't fit? (Yes)
>
> . . . come from surfers and dealers but not from our own Quality Control? (Yes)
>
> . . . come from Florida and California but not from the Northeast? (No!)

As soon as you hit a No, you know the theory has a weakness and isn't as reliable as one that fits *all* the facts of the problem. In Jack's case, it's quite clear that if materials *alone* were the cause of the warping, then there should be complaints from *all* areas. This logical check-out not only shows that Jack's first theory is a poor bet as it stands, but also points us in a useful direction: we now see that *no* theory that doesn't include some difference between the regions as part of its causal pattern will satisfy our logical test in this case. This shoots down the third (storage) theory, too.

With only one theory left, it's very tempting to accept it at face value instead of honestly trying to shoot it down along with the others. It takes real self-discipline to put your only remaining possibility to the test. But would you rather find out two months and $10,000 later that this one was also a false lead?

Causes Aren't Corrections

Jack's second theory (warping by Southern heat on the STUD) appears to fit all the known facts of the problem. This information *doesn't* tell Jack what corrective action to take, but it will help in his search for alternatives and in selecting the most reliable and feasible among them. As we saw in Chapters 4 to 6, however, there are many other things that also need to be considered. The most probable cause is only one very helpful "input" to the decision.

It should also be noted that the method of analysis we have illustrated above can be applied to *positive* deviations (where things went *better* than planned) just as well as to negative ones. In my opinion, this is its most promising and underdeveloped application. Every industrial and business process varies around a standard. Managers typically get excited and launch investigations when performance falls *below* standard, but sit back and smile when it is above. If positive deviations were investigated with equal vigor, performance could be maintained nearer the peaks to which it occasionally swings.

Deviation Analysis versus Research

Managers and scientists both solve problems. Their objectives, however, are very different. The scientific researcher wants to add knowledge. Each time he isolates a set of causal factors, he immediately wonders what other factors caused those causes! For example, if a scientist concludes that smoking can cause cancer, he doesn't stop there. He wants to find out what elements in tobacco are responsible. If he finds that it appears to be the tar, then he wants to find out *why* tar has this effect on man.

In a sense, the true researcher gets his kicks out of working at a task he knows he can never finish. There are always causes behind causes, in an endless chain of relationships. All any one scientist can do in his entire lifetime is push our understanding a little farther along this endless chain.

Managers, on the other hand, are interested in results and profits. Since problem solving takes time and people, it is an item of cost. Therefore, managers should want as *little* of it as they can get away with and still keep ahead of the competition. This point sets a major goal for any system of deviation analysis to be used by managers: *efficiency*. To be useful, the approach must strike a balance between the need to pin down causes and the need to get on with the business.

Striking the Balance

Knowing when to *stop* a deviation analysis can be just as important as knowing when to start it. There are two criteria that every manager understands to guide you in making this judgment: risk and cost. These two factors can keep your problem solving practical. As an operating manager, you don't need any more analysis of a deviation than it takes to visualize a safe-enough and cheap-enough corrective course of action. Competitive pressures make deeper research unjustified.

How can you tell when you've gone far enough? Usually, a manager's general background knowledge about his operation and its budget will be sufficient guide. When doubt remains, the best known way to check whether further analysis is advisable is to push just *one* step farther and see if any significantly safer or cheaper action ideas are produced. If not, drop the analysis and get on with the action!

You're the Analyst

Here's a chance to flex your muscles as a deviation analyst. The problem, though homey, is real. It caused a lot of discomfort and could have cost a lot of money. Furthermore, it could happen to you. In any case, the fact that it happened, and was solved, gives us the advantage of knowing the actual cause and at least one effective corrective action.

First I'll tell you all I knew about the problem up to the moment that it became so intolerable I had to do something about it. Then I invite you to apply deviation analysis to the information and see what you come up with in the way of causes. Finally, I'll show you how I applied the process and how the problem was solved.

"Don't Flush, I'm in the Shower!"

That's my name for the problem, and here's the history. When we built the house, 13 years ago, the 210-foot-deep artesian well tested out at a steady flow of 27 gallons per minute, which is far above the minimum needed for a private dwelling. With the submersed pump and pressure tank, our system maintained a 60-pound-per-square-inch maximum and a 40-pound-per-square-inch minimum pressure. This was enough to do the dishes, flush the toilet, and still maintain satisfactory pressure in the shower. With three bathrooms and four children, that is important!

We soon found that our water was very hard and left a brown deposit in the toilets that was difficult to remove. A water-softening system was installed. This gave us a lovely, sudsy water and significantly reduced the brown deposit.

The well was a blessing during the year of the water shortage. While others were prohibited from washing cars and watering lawns, we had all the water we wanted. Our well, which is the deepest in the neighborhood, continued to produce even when some of the shallower ones ran low. At one point we ran a hose over to a neighbor's who was getting nothing but a little mud from his faucets. He eventually had to replace his pump and part of his plumbing.

Then came the thruway. They made a deep cut in solid rock for an access road just beyond our next-door neighbor and opened up a spring in the process. Apparently, they had cut through an upper layer of the water table. Our neighbor's well ran dry and he had to have a completely new one drilled. It was located near our property line, and they had to go down to 200 feet before getting an adequate flow.

Over the years, our flow of water lessened. I checked the gauge on the pressure tank from time to time, and it continued to give readings between 40 and 60 pounds per square inch. Nevertheless, the actual flow from our faucets became inadequate. Three features of the problem made us slow to react:

■ When no other water was being drawn, the flow from any one outlet wasn't bad.

■ When any outlet was first turned on, the flow came with fair force.

■ The whole problem came on gradually, over a long period of time.

Cleanliness is next to. . . .

It happened in the shower. I had just gotten all lathered up and was stepping back in to rinse. The water turned cold for an instant and then stopped altogether. I yelled, but it was too late: my wife had started a wash cycle and my son had flushed the toilet. It would be about five minutes before my shower would begin to trickle cold water, and I had to get to work.

I sent my wife with a pot to all the different faucets in the house, hoping for enough water to at least rinse my face. No luck. I had her try the outside hose outlet, on the theory that since these lines joined the main feed line just a few feet from the pressure tank and in front of the water-softening system, they would be most likely to produce. She did get a slow trickle there and poured a panful of cold water over my head. I got soap in my eyes and she got some advice on when not to start a wash. I got some enlightenment on why she started it so early: the water problem caused the machine to take almost twice as long to go through its cycle. At that point, still cold and soapy in the shower, I began to analyze the problem while I waited for the return of a little pressure.

Now you have all the facts and some of the feelings. You're probably dry and warm, too, so you are in a lot better shape to think about the whole thing. My only concern is that you may not be quite as highly motivated as I was!

Before you look at my analysis that follows, take a sheet of paper and define the deviation for yourself. Then look for differences, changes, and possible causes. Test your various possible causes against the definition of the deviation and see what action you would take.

The Deviation Defined

Water Pressure Problem

Reported	*Not reported*
ITEM: Inadequate pressure	If only one outlet used
Toilets slow to refill	

Water Pressure Problem (*Continued*)

Reported	Not reported
Washing machine cycle slow	
Flow may stop altogether	
SOURCE: All family members	
Guests	
PLACE: All outlets	At pressure tank gauge
Outside hose bib, too	
TIME: Whenever more than one outlet in use	When house was new
	When faucet first turned on
Any time of day or night	
Gradually getting worse over the years	Prior to about 5 years ago
AMOUNT: Wash cycle twice as long	Precise reduction in flow
	Rate of decrease after faucet turned on
5 minutes to refill toilet	

I have to confess that even in my hour of analysis and repair, I did some sloppy thinking. Before really defining the deviation, I angrily considered some alternatives and their probable costs:

- Move ($?????)
- A new well ($2,000)
- Bring in city water ($2,500)
- A new pump ($350)
- A new pressure tank ($500)
- New water softener ($125)
- Replace clogged pipes throughout ($1,500)

However, the definition narrowed the problem down. Since the tank pressure gauge showed normal readings and the actual initial pressure was fine, the pump obviously was capable of building up adequate pressure in the tank; and the tank could hold it. The fact that pressure dropped as soon as a second outlet was turned on (and *before* the tank could have run low on water) suggested that the problem was not with the supply from the well. The fact that even the hose bib also had the problem proved that the softener wasn't the main cause, and that whatever the cause was, it could operate in the few feet of pipe between the pressure tank and the hose bib.

What could cut down the flow of water in that short section of pipe, also affecting all the rest of the house, and still leave the entire system so the initial spurt would be at full pressure? Could it be that the brown sediment which had bothered us only for its appearance actually built up over the years on the inside of the pipes and gradually restricted the flow of water? This would not harm the initial pressure, nor would the buildup be as bad beyond the softener. It would be worst *before* the softener, but this would still affect the entire system.

A Cheap Test

The theory might or might not be correct, but at least there was a quick, simple, and safe way to test it. Making sure the tank was up to full pressure, I opened up the hose bib as far as it would go and ran back into the basement with a small sledge to beat on the pressure tank near the outlet and all along the main feed line. My wife, who was watching the hose, yelled and I ran out to look: there was a thick, reddish-brown stream pouring out! I ran back, continued my smart raps on the feed pipe, and then let the hose run for about fifteen minutes.

Archimedes is supposed to have sung out his "Eureka!" in the tub, when he figured out that flotation was caused by displacement of water. Well, that was nothing compared to my "Wha-hoo!" in the shower when I confirmed my theory that feed-pipe flagellation produced a full-force water supply, *with* another shower going *and* a toilet flushing.

Let me tell you: my wife was quite impressed. That was over a year ago, and I haven't had to beat my pipes since.

Back to Process

Note that in this case, I didn't march systematically through all the steps of identifying differences, looking for changes, and then developing causal theories. Once the deviation was defined, I immediately began eliminating possible causes that I had been considering *before* I'd ever stopped to organize my information into a structured definition of the deviation. This will often happen and there's nothing wrong with it *as long as you know what you're doing.*

My point is that while I think the method of dealing with deviations that has been described above is a very good one, I know it isn't the *only* one and I'm sure there will be *better* ones in the future. What is much less likely to change is *the great value of becoming conscious of process*. It's the best general method I know for keeping things, including yourself, under control.

Applied to Teamwork

As a manager, you'll rarely have the luxury of being able to wipe the soap out of your eyes, mentally gather up all the information on a problem, and methodically work through a deviation analysis. Most of the serious problems you encounter will have information spread all over the place and many different kinds of people involved. Your task will be to *manage* the problem solving, rather than solve the problem yourself. This, unquestionably, is much more difficult.

Of course you'll have the authority to tell people what to do, but *what* will you tell them to do? "I want this cleared up by 9 A.M. tomorrow," is one approach. The trouble with this approach is that you haven't really helped the problem solver, nor have you added to your own assurance that the problem will be solved. If you want to be more specific and less threatening, the process we've just practiced offers an outline.

1. *List deviations* from plan.
2. *Set priorities* to decide which comes first.
3. *Define* the top-priority deviation.
4. Identify *differences.*
5. List *changes* in the differences.
6. Develop *possible causes.*
7. *Test possible causes* logically against the definition.
8. Run *operating tests* on the most probable causes.
9. Design *corrective alternatives.*
10. *Evaluate* corrective alternatives.

Solving for Today versus Tomorrow

If the next problem that comes up threatens the whole future of your operation and you're convinced no one else can handle it satisfactorily, you'll certainly take over, using whatever approach you trust most. This will be understood and respected, providing the circumstances are truly critical and you *are* the appropriate party to take over. It will be particularly appreciated if, once the crisis is past, you explain to everyone involved *why* you took such a strong hand and *how* you structured your attack on the problem.

This kind of extreme threat is rare, however, and you should become suspicious if deviations from plan look this way very often. In most cases, others can do a perfectly good job; and in some, they will do better than you could, if they get the chance. But as the manager you are still responsible, and therefore you must maintain control even though you want to encourage team problem solving.

The best way to manage a deviation analysis and to delegate and build team problem-solving skills is with the use of *questions.* Questions are the only way I know to control without directing; to teach without lecturing. To be effective, the questions should follow a conscious, logical process that fits the situation at hand. In this case, the ten steps of deviation analysis form an excellent outline for questioning.

1. *List deviations:*
   What *other* problems do we face just now?
   Who else might know if this is our only problem?

2. *Set priorities:*
   Which problem should we tackle first?
   How did you decide where to begin?
   Are there any other factors we ought to consider in setting priorities?

3. *Define:*
   Is this the *only* complaint?
   Can you be more specific about the complaint?
   Who is complaining?
   Where do the complaints come from?
   When did they begin?
   How many have we had?
   Are we missing any useful information?
   Are you sure this information is accurate?

4. *Differences:*
   What is different about where we have the problem as opposed to where we don't?
   What's different about the malfunctioning unit versus the other parts?

5. *Changes:*
   How can we select which changes we ought to take a close look at?
   Do these differences you've noted suggest any recent changes?

6. *Causes:*
   What's the best basis for a causal theory?
   Should causes include only changes?
   Who would be a good source for ideas about causes on a problem like this?

7. *Logical test:*

How can we test this idea without lots of time and unnecessary expense?

How does that cause fit in with what we already know about the problem?

8. *Operating test:*

   How can we positively verify that the fix will work?

   Does the test adequately simulate field conditions?

   How will you judge whether the test is a success or failure?

9. *Corrective alternatives:*

   What guides do you plan to use in developing possible alternatives?

   How many will you want to consider?

   Who should be involved in this activity?

10. *Evaluation:*

    What criteria will be used?

    Who will make the best judges?

    How will you try to protect against oversights?

These are just samples to get you started. Once you begin to develop the art of asking questions, you'll think of many more. This happens because asking quesions is usually followed by listening for answers, and the act of listening tends to open the mind. An open mind is the most important requirement for learning and managing.[24]

Exercise in Teamwork

In Appendix 1, you will find a problem presented so you can practice *managing* a deviation analysis. I strongly recommend that you find three other interested parties (they could even be members of your family) and try to apply some of the recommendations of this chapter to the exercise. The case contains instructions and all the information needed for a good workout on team problem solving.

Appendix 2 contains the analysis of the problem, worked out according to the process described in this chapter.

IN SUMMARY

This chapter has dealt with the fifth and final phase of our management method: deviation analysis. Resistance to systematic approaches of problem analysis was recognized. One highly structured method was presented through case example, with a second real situation for practice application. Implications of the method for team problem solving were examined, and a sample list of questions was offered to help managers maintain control and still stimulate people to creativity and teamwork in solving problems.

chapter 9

Ready to Manage

IF YOU'RE BECOMING AT ALL SENSITIVE TO METHOD, as opposed to content, you've noticed that each of the last five chapters has the same basic structure. First comes a discussion of a process for organizing and manipulating a particular kind of information. This is followed by recommendations on how to involve and manage other people effectively when dealing with that kind of information. These are seen as two distinguishable but closely related activities. A logical information process won't go far if the people involved don't understand and support it. Conversely, I believe that a lot of goodwill can end in confusion and frustration if rational guidance is lacking. Ideally, this guidance comes from the manager *and* the managed.

While everyone can help improve both the information and the motivational process in any given work situation, final responsibility lies with the manager. Two characteristics are essential for adequate and consistent fulfillment of these responsibilities. A manager must:

■ Understand and apply the distinction between "content" and "process";

■ Be eager to learn.

The value, particularly for managing, of an open mind has been discussed. The distinction between *what* is done, as opposed to *how* it is done, is essential for managing at all organization levels. There are times, especially in crisis, when a manager will have to deal directly with work content. There are times, especially in training, when he should emphasize process. There are times, such as appraisal, when he will want to examine both. The key is to have a conscious plan for which to consider when, and why.

Managing Managers

This sensitivity to process versus content has special significance as you climb the organization ladder. To make the point, let me borrow a much-used diagram that represents, in simplified form, what managers at different organization levels actually *do*.

Level	Activity
	Work Managing
Second-level manager:	▢▨▨▨▨▨▨
First-level manager:	▢▨▨▨
Worker:	▢▨

The increasing amount of managing and decreasing amount of individual functional work that characterizes higher organization levels has direct implications for managing: the higher the level the more a manager manages his subordinate's *managing,* as opposed to his individual work.

What's the best approach to managing another manager's managing? I believe the focus should be on his methods and general approach rather than on detail. He's much more likely to see the logic underlying your recommendations and to apply them in many situations rather than just the one that stimulated your observation. Also, it helps *him* become more conscious of process, and thereby puts him in a better position to evaluate and improve himself.

Managing Young People

Perhaps the most critical long-range problem facing managers is the changing attitudes of young people toward authority. It appears that there is less and less readiness to accept authority based solely on age or organizational position. Whatever the causes and proprieties of this trend, the consequences must be faced: managers will increasingly have to depend upon other resources for their authority.

Even the threat of dismissal is losing its potency. In our age of affluence, many people of all ages are quite ready to change jobs: so much so that managers are often more concerned with how to hold people than how to get rid of them.

This puts managers in a difficult position. They must maintain control, and they must hold turnover to reasonable levels; yet their power of position is being constantly eroded. Is there any solid foundation for authority that remains?

The thesis of this book is that sensitivity to process and skill in applying methods of managing information and stimulating motivation are valid and durable sources of leadership authority. I believe they will command respect wherever practiced and will become even more highly prized as the world becomes more and more crowded and complicated.

The Problem

The following problem involved many people and a lot of money. I've concealed identities and consolidated all the essential information into four separate positions. This makes it possible for several people to tackle the situation and use it as an exercise in team deviation analysis.

To gain practice in *managing* a deviation analysis, I suggest you read *only* the section entitled "General Manager." Have three other individuals each read only one of the other positions. (If you can only find two associates, have one of them take both the Manufacturing and Quality Control materials.) Each set of materials has an introductory general statement that is the same for everyone, followed by letters and interoffice memoranda sent or received by the individual in that particular position. Thus when you get together after having read your material, you and your associates will have some information in common, and each of you may know some things unknown to any of the others. Your assignment is to do whatever you judge to be in the best interests of the company.

Procedurally, there are two things that can add greatly to your learning from this exercise:

1. As general manager, use a standing easel chart or blackboard so everyone can see the record of everyone's contributions to the analysis.

2. Tape record your discussions so you can review them later.

As a team, you should allow yourselves about one hour to analyze this problem after you've read the material. Do not read Appendix 2 until you've completed your analysis. Also, do not read each other's material. Accept all unquoted statements in the case as factual. Beware of adding information that you or your associates think would probably be true but may have been omitted.

One other thing: have some fun; see if you can save Gale!

GALE LOCKS

Gale Locks, Inc., produces a variety of doorlocks, padlocks, small safes, and other security devices. Through its padlock division, Gale has enjoyed the lion's share of the national padlock market for half a century. Simple, sturdy design, plus meticulous quality control have earned Gale a reputation for reliability and durability. This quality image plus the universal public awareness of Gale as "the biggest and oldest lockmaker in the business" are considered the major reasons for Gale's ability to hold higher prices and continue to build market share over the years.

During the last decade, however, competition has intensified. Several smaller manufacturers have produced padlocks of practically identical appearance to Gale's, but priced 20 to 40 percent lower. While relatively few hardware stores or locksmiths have discontinued the Gale lines, almost all outlets have taken on one or more competitive lines with the result that Gale sales in both its padlock lines have been affected. For three years, until about a year ago, the growth rate went into sharp decline in spite of massive advertising campaigns and sales contests—both of which represented quite a depar-

ture for the old firm. Another blow has been the advent of supermarkets and discount houses as an outlet for hardware items, including padlocks. Hardly any of these new outlets have taken on the Gale lines.

For several years Gale marketing and sales pleaded for a third new line that would be price competitive with the padlocks sold at discount houses. Until recently, top management resisted on grounds that the Gale image would be damaged and their quality lines would suffer. However, when T. Frothingham Gale, Jr., took over the reins from "Old Frothy" eighteen months ago, one of his first directives was to set up a new, low-priced padlock. As anticipated by Marketing and Sales, this new line—very similar in appearance to Gale's "middle-priced" line and bearing the Gale monogram—exceeded expectations during its first year on the market. Furthermore, sales of the new line have not, as yet, had any visible effect on the two higher-priced lines.

Manufacturing procedure for padlocks varies with quality. Gale buys the brass case for its A line (top-quality padlock) from an outside manufacturer. The lock cores (all internal locking parts) are machined from raw brass stock, rubbed with dry graphite for permanent lubrication, assembled into the cases together with the shackles (steel wire shaped in a die), and riveted in place with two pins. The padlocks are then polished, sprayed with clear lacquer, stamped with the Gale monogram, the monogram letters are paint-filled, and the finished lock is packaged.

Gale makes its own B line cases. Extruded brass bar stock is cut off, drilled, and completely machined in a Kingsbury machine. The remainder of the B line procedure is the same as the A line—the primary difference between the two lines being the greater weight and strength of the A line locks. (Each line comes in two sizes.)

The new 206 (also two sizes) is a zinc die-cast padlock. In sequence, the procedures are casting, broaching, drilling, finishing (buffing followed by anticorrosion nickel-chrome plating), assembling (core and steel wire shackle into the case), silver painting, and packaging.

The primary bottleneck in the A and B lines was always the individual rubbing of lock cores in dry graphite. In order to achieve the much greater volume required of the 206 line, a new method of lubrication has been developed by Engineering: the lock cores are left in their large tray holders, used in plating, dipped in a heated solution containing graphite in suspension, and then conveyed through an oven that bakes the residue of graphite onto the core surfaces. This eliminates individual handling of each lock core and realizes a significant labor savings. The new procedure has run smoothly and is presently being evaluated by Quality Control for application on the old A and B lines.

Subsequent developments at Gale will be presented in the form in which the information was actually communicated.* For our purposes, it will be most interesting to examine these events from the point of view of the General Manager of the Padlock Division and those functional managers reporting to him: Sales, Manufacturing, and Quality Control. The date today is Tuesday, July 20, 1965.

January 14, 1965

MEMORANDUM TO: General Manager, Padlock Division
SUBJECT: Anticipated Krinland Price Hike

The following quotation from Krinland Sales is self-explanatory:

"This is to inform you that we anticipate no further problem on delivery of 7/32-inch steel wire for your shackle operation. We must point out, however, that rising costs will almost certainly dictate a price renegotiation when our present contract terminates. You can

---

* For those unfamiliar with padlock nomenclature:
  CORE: all locking parts contained inside the case.
  PLUG: part of the core; the cylindrical, rotating part into which the key is inserted.
  SHACKLE: the movable steel wire loop that is partially released when padlock is unlocked.

be sure that the new price will be competitive and that Krinland quality will—as always—be tops."

I'm lining up alternate suppliers of $7/32$- and $1/4$-inch wire.

Purchasing

March 19, 1965

MEMORANDUM TO: General Manager, Padlock Division
SUBJECT: Revision of Test Procedures

We are currently revising our procedures on the shackle tolerance test. Shackle bending has always been a critical area, due to variations in skin hardness and age of wire. Final adjustments (tapping, pinching, spreading) are often required and take considerable operator skill.

Since any defect in shackle fit has a direct effect on lock function, we have decided to go from 10 percent to a 25 percent sampling on shackle test for at least the next quarter. We're going to try to accomplish this without an increase in personnel; but if thi: ʌroves to be impossible, we feel the additional cost will be justified. Gale has been built on a foundation of quality, and we're not about to let anybody undermine that!

Quality Control

March 29, 1965

MEMORANDUM TO: General Manager, Padlock Division
SUBJECT: Progress Report on 206 Line

As of the end of last week we are now meeting the 206 production schedule. Judging by the way things are running, we should have no problem continuing to do so. We had to break in some new hands on the shackle operation during the last couple of weeks, but everyone's up to quota now. Since we are now at full volume on the line, any significant increase in the schedule will either require going to three shifts or expanding our facilities.

Quality Control is still working on test standards, but this represents no problem for us since the new line runs like clockwork and produces a damn good lock.

Manufacturing

May 18, 1965

MEMORANDUM TO: General Manager, Padlock Division
SUBJECT: New Packaging

We now have a three-months' supply of the new lighter boxes and cartons for the 206s, and our supplier assures us there is no supply problem for the foreseeable future. As of June 1 we'll be shipping all 206s in the new packaging.

Packaging and Shipping

May 25, 1965

MEMORANDUM TO: General Manager, Padlock Division
SUBJECT: Effective Communications

If you haven't already done so, I would like to suggest that it might be advisable for you to communicate our pleasure over the first year's results with the 206 to the keymen involved with the development and implementation of this major and obviously sound decision that currently gives every indication of producing a major breakthrough with respect to the market position of our key product line.

T. F. Gale, Jr.

FILE COPY

June 1, 1965

MEMORANDUM TO: Manufacturing
SUBJECT: Congratulations!

Congratulations on your first year's 206 production. I want you to know that T. F., Jr., and I are duly impressed with the way you got this new line rolling and more recently with the production levels you've reached and held without loss of quality.

On that score, a special note is due Quality Control for continuing to see to it that Gale customers only get the good ones. That's how we keep 'em locked in on Gale!

General Manager, Padlock Division

cc: Quality Control

FILE COPY

June 1, 1965

MEMORANDUM TO: Marketing and Sales
SUBJECT: Congratulations!

I want to take this occasion to congratulate you gentlemen on our first year's success with the new 206 line. T. F., Jr., and I recognize that it was you two who really sparked this decision, and you've both had a major hand in making it a good one—beyond our original expectations.

I also wanted to give you early notice that we'll almost certainly raise our quota 20 percent on the 206s for next quarter. I'm betting on Sales to beat that one, too!

General Manager, Padlock Division

June 3, 1965

MEMORANDUM TO: General Manager, Padlock Division
SUBJECT: Conversion to Hot Dip

Apparently promoting Susy MacDonald to Quality Control last March had a good effect all around. Marge Jensen, for example, was always considered marginal on lubrication, but since she's had it all to herself with the new hot-dip procedure, she's going great guns. The men down in plating tell me Marge is always ready for them when they bring up the core trays. I checked with Marge herself recently and her only comment was, "No sweat!"

I go into this because I think it's high time we converted to hot dip on A and B lines. I don't know why Quality Control is dragging its feet on this one. Every day we dry-rub is just more dollars down the drain!

Manufacturing

July 20, 1965

MEMORANDUM TO: General Manager, Padlock Division
SUBJECT: New Policy on Promotions

We would like to question the universal applicability of our current practice of promoting top performers regardless of personality and background. The fact that Susy MacDonald appears to have made the switch over to Quality Control does not, in our mind, prove the principle.

In a sense, Susy had everything going for her. The difference between dry-rubbing cores and testing keys and shackle fit is not great. Also, she happens to be the kind of girl everybody likes. Consider, though, the probable consequences of trying to put someone like that in a managerial position!

I would appreciate an opportunity to review this matter with you in depth at your convenience. I consider it urgent, since serious misplacements could occur if we let this slide. Actually, it is our moral responsibility to our people to make sure we are placing them to the best of our ability.

Personnel

cc: Manufacturing

GALE LOCKS

Gale Locks, Inc., produces a variety of doorlocks, padlocks, small safes, and other security devices. Through its padlock division, Gale has enjoyed the lion's share of the national padlock market for half a century. Simple, sturdy design, plus meticulous quality control have earned Gale a reputation for reliability and durability. This quality image plus the universal public awareness of Gale as "the biggest and oldest lockmaker in the business" are considered the major reasons for Gale's ability to hold higher prices and continue to build market share over the years.

During the last decade, however, competition has intensified. Several smaller manufacturers have produced padlocks of practically identical appearance to Gale's, but priced 20 to 40 percent lower. While relatively few hardware stores or locksmiths have discontinued the Gale lines, almost all outlets have taken on one or more competitive lines with the result that Gale sales in both its padlock lines have been affected. For three years, until about a year ago, the growth rate went into sharp decline in spite of massive advertising campaigns and sales contests—both of which represented quite a depar-

ture for the old firm. Another blow has been the advent of supermarkets and discount houses as an outlet for hardware items, including padlocks. Hardly any of these new outlets have taken on the Gale lines.

For several years Gale marketing and sales pleaded for a third new line that would be price competitive with the padlocks sold at discount houses. Until recently, top management resisted on grounds that the Gale image would be damaged and their quality lines would suffer. However, when T. Frothingham Gale, Jr., took over the reins from "Old Frothy" eighteen months ago, one of his first directives was to set up a new, low-priced padlock. As anticipated by Marketing and Sales, this new line—very similar in appearance to Gale's "middle-priced" line and bearing the Gale monogram—exceeded expectations during its first year on the market. Furthermore, sales of the new line have not, as yet, had any visible effect on the two higher-priced lines.

Manufacturing procedure for padlocks varies with quality. Gale buys the brass case for its A line (top-quality padlock) from an outside manufacturer. The lock cores (all internal locking parts) are machined from raw brass stock, rubbed with dry graphite for permanent lubrication, assembled into the cases together with the shackles (steel wire shaped in a die), and riveted in place with two pins. The padlocks are then polished, sprayed with clear lacquer, stamped with the Gale monogram, the monogram letters are paint-filled, and the finished lock is packaged.

Gale makes its own B line cases. Extruded brass bar stock is cut off, drilled, and completely machined in a Kingsbury machine. The remainder of the B line procedure is the same as the A line—the primary difference between the two lines being the greater weight and strength of the A line locks. (Each line comes in two sizes.)

The new 206 (also two sizes) is a zinc die-cast padlock. In sequence, the procedures are casting, broaching, drilling, finishing (buffing followed by anticorrosion nickel-chrome plating), assembling (core and steel wire shackle into the case), silver painting, and packaging.

The primary bottleneck in the A and B lines was always the individual rubbing of lock cores in dry graphite. In order to achieve the much greater volume required of the 206 line, a new method of lubrication has been developed by Engineering: the lock cores are left in their large tray holders, used in plating, dipped in a heated solution containing graphite in suspension, and then conveyed through an oven that bakes the residue of graphite onto the core surfaces. This eliminates individual handling of each lock core and realizes a significant labor savings. The new procedure has run smoothly and is presently being evaluated by Quality Control for application on the old A and B lines.

Subsequent developments at Gale will be presented in the form in which the information was actually communicated.* For our purposes, it will be most interesting to examine these events from the point of view of the General Manager of the Padlock Division and those functional managers reporting to him: Sales, Manufacturing, and Quality Control. The date today is Tuesday, July 20, 1965.

January 4, 1965

MEMORANDUM TO: Sales
SUBJECT: Six Months with the 206

I've just finished reviewing the preliminary figures you sent over on our first six months with the 206, and I'd say the picture looks pretty good. I don't like to count my chickens before they're hatched, but if you project our first half year's growth on the new line it now looks like we'll beat our June target by a very healthy margin.

---

* For those unfamiliar with padlock nomenclature:
  CORE: all locking parts contained inside the case.
  PLUG: part of the core; the cylindrical, rotating part into which the key is inserted.
  SHACKLE: the movable steel wire loop that is partially released when padlock is unlocked.

I've been beating my brains out trying to anticipate what might happen to slow us down in the next six months; but short of a strike in production, I think we're in the clear. I'll keep my fingers crossed and give some thought to an appropriate celebration. How does Friday, June 4, sound to you?

Marketing

April 5, 1965

MEMORANDUM TO: Sales
SUBJECT: First Quarter Sales, Eastern Region

I'm sending you, under separate cover, a complete breakdown of our first quarter sales. At this point, I'd just like to net out certain points:

1. The Eastern region is 18 percent over quota for the first quarter.
2. This healthy state of affairs is due entirely to our success with the 206 (you will note that the A and B lines have continued along the same unfortunate trend that was established long before we brought on the 206).
3. We have obtained more new accounts in this quarter than my region has obtained in any quarter of Gale's history.

Field Sales Manager, Eastern Region

May 20, 1965

MEMORANDUM TO: Sales
SUBJECT: A and B Sales

Chief, I am very concerned about the recent history of our good old A and B lines. Frankly, I think we're all letting the 206—which I wouldn't knock for the world—blind us to the very serious problem that continues to face us in our quality lines. Let's not forget that it was *quality*—at a fair price—that built Gale.

Personally, I'm convinced that as income levels continue to rise there will be a swing back to quality as a key element required by consumers of hardware items. This is the reason I think it is so important for us to maintain our quality image.

I recommend that we try everything in our power (short of price-cutting) to reverse the trend on our A and B lines. Maybe a sales contest, or an advertising campaign underscoring the greater security of a quality padlock. Marketing ought to be able to help us on this one.

Field Sales Manager, Western Region

June 1, 1965

MEMORANDUM TO: Marketing and <u>Sales</u>
SUBJECT: Congratulations!

I want to take this occasion to congratulate you gentlemen on our first year's success with the new 206 line. T. F., Jr., and I recognize that it was you two who really sparked this decision, and you've both had a major hand in making it a good one—beyond our original expectations.

I also wanted to give you early notice that we'll almost certainly raise our quota 20 percent on the 206s for next quarter. I'm betting on Sales to beat that one, too!

General Manager, Padlock Division

July 1, 1965

MEMORANDUM TO: Sales
SUBJECT: First Anniversary of the 206

Not that I'm surprised, but it was pleasing to go over the first year's figures you sent me on the 206 and see just how well we've done. I always felt the concept of a more competitively priced quality padlock was sound, in spite of all the flak we got from the old-timers. Aren't you and I a little overdue for a celebration? If you've got the time, I've got the place!

Marketing

July 5, 1965

MEMORANDUM TO: Sales
SUBJECT: New Accounts Progress Report

I just wanted you to know that as of this writing it looks like we'll land Korvette, which will put us way over quota for the entire quarter. The only dark spot on the entire horizon is a couple of minor complaints two of my men picked up last week. Two hardware store managers—one in Stamford, Connecticut, and the other down in Charleston, South Carolina—passed on some customer complaints about our new locks freezing up.

The Stamford man said his customer—a big-time yachtsman—reported that a shot of penetrating oil solved the problem. You can imagine how I hit the roof when I heard that one! I sat down immediately and wrote the store manager telling him how important it is to *never* oil a Gale. I explained to him how this collects fine sediment and soon ruins the lock, and recommended that he warn his customers against ever oiling one of our locks. I also reminded him of our long-standing policy of immediate replacement on any returned lock found to have a manufacturing defect, though we've had practically no cases of this to my knowledge.

I'll keep you posted on the Korvette deal.

Field Sales Manager, Eastern Region

July 8, 1965

MEMORANDUM TO: Sales
SUBJECT: Customer Complaints

Chief, we've got a crisis brewing out here that requires some prompt action! What the hell's gone wrong in Manufacturing? We're getting snowed with complaints that our locks freeze up—within a few weeks after purchase. I've got some nasty letters from dealers in Seattle and Los Angeles, and we're beginning to hurt on new orders.

I'll do my best to pour oil on the troubled waters, but you better tell Manufacturing to speed up the 206 line if we're ever going to make good on our replacement policy. I anticipate having one hell of a load of replacement requests in the near future. And for heaven's sake let's be sure there's nothing wrong with the replacements!

Field Sales Manager, Western Region

FILE COPY

July 8, 1965

MEMORANDUM TO: Manufacturing and Quality Control
SUBJECT: Customer Complaints of Frozen Locks

Gentlemen, something has gone very wrong with our new padlock line. We've been getting a lot of customer complaints to the effect that our locks freeze up and can't be opened unless penetrating oil is used. From what I've been able to gather, the plugs won't turn—even when enough force is exerted to break off the key. In other cases they claim they can't even get the key all the way into the plug.

I won't insult you with any theories as to what's causing this problem but I will offer this observation: There'll be more than one kind of Gale around here if this isn't cleared up—like now!

I'll forward our estimates on replacement requirements as soon as we have more specific information on the extent of the problem.

Sales

July 9, 1965

MEMORANDUM TO: Sales
SUBJECT: The Korvette Account

We've had some bad luck: Our contact at E. J. Korvette got wind of the complaints we've been having lately—which have continued to come in since I last wrote you. Well, to get to the point, the Korvette buyer told us he'll go Corbin unless we get a fast fix on this freezing problem.

Need I say more?

Field Sales Manager, Eastern Region

July 12, 1965

MEMORANDUM TO: Sales
SUBJECT: 206 Complaints

I'm very sorry to learn about your problem. Fortunately, I can assure you that everything is running smoothly in manufacturing—so much so that I certainly hope these complaints get nailed before any of my people hear about it. We've had quite a struggle getting up to schedule on the new line, and the last thing I need now is an investigation!

Incidently, I do happen to know that shipping made some changes in packaging a month or so ago, as part of our campaign to cut costs. This might bear investigation. Then there's always an outside chance that Quality Control let a few rough ones past. I doubt this, but we always have—and probably always will have—variability in the shackle fit due to variations in metallurgical characteristics of the raw shackle wire.

Manufacturing

GALE LOCKS

Gale Locks, Inc., produces a variety of doorlocks, padlocks, small safes, and other security devices. Through its padlock division, Gale has enjoyed the lion's share of the national padlock market for half a century. Simple, sturdy design, plus meticulous quality control have earned Gale a reputation for reliability and durability. This quality image plus the universal public awareness of Gale as "the biggest and oldest lockmaker in the business" are considered the major reasons for Gale's ability to hold higher prices and continue to build market share over the years.

During the last decade, however, competition has intensified. Several smaller manufacturers have produced padlocks of practically identical appearance to Gale's, but priced 20 to 40 percent lower. While relatively few hardware stores or locksmiths have discontinued the Gale lines, almost all outlets have taken on one or more competitive lines with the result that Gale sales in both its padlock lines have been affected. For three years, until about a year ago, the growth rate went into sharp decline in spite of massive advertising campaigns and sales contests—both of which represented quite a depar-

ture for the old firm. Another blow has been the advent of supermarkets and discount houses as an outlet for hardware items, including padlocks. Hardly any of these new outlets have taken on the Gale lines.

For several years Gale marketing and sales pleaded for a third new line that would be price competitive with the padlocks sold at discount houses. Until recently, top management resisted on grounds that the Gale image would be damaged and their quality lines would suffer. However, when T. Frothingham Gale, Jr., took over the reins from "Old Frothy" eighteen months ago, one of his first directives was to set up a new, low-priced padlock. As anticipated by Marketing and Sales, this new line—very similar in appearance to Gale's "middle-priced" line and bearing the Gale monogram—exceeded expectations during its first year on the market. Furthermore, sales of the new line have not, as yet, had any visible effect on the two higher-priced lines.

Manufacturing procedure for padlocks varies with quality. Gale buys the brass case for its A line (top-quality padlock) from an outside manufacturer. The lock cores (all internal locking parts) are machined from raw brass stock, rubbed with dry graphite for permanent lubrication, assembled into the cases together with the shackles (steel wire shaped in a die), and riveted in place with two pins. The padlocks are then polished, sprayed with clear lacquer, stamped with the Gale monogram, the monogram letters are paint-filled, and the finished lock is packaged.

Gale makes its own B line cases. Extruded brass bar stock is cut off, drilled, and completely machined in a Kingsbury machine. The remainder of the B line procedure is the same as the A line—the primary difference between the two lines being the greater weight and strength of the A line locks. (Each line comes in two sizes.)

The new 206 (also two sizes) is a zinc die-cast padlock. In sequence, the procedures are casting, broaching, drilling, finishing (buffing followed by anticorrosion nickel-chrome plating), assembling (core and steel wire shackle into the case), silver painting, and packaging.

The primary bottleneck in the A and B lines was always the individual rubbing of lock cores in dry graphite. In order to achieve the much greater volume required of the 206 line, a new method of lubrication has been developed by Engineering: the lock cores are left in their large tray holders, used in plating, dipped in a heated solution containing graphite in suspension, and then conveyed through an oven that bakes the residue of graphite onto the core surfaces. This eliminates individual handling of each lock core and realizes a significant labor savings. The new procedure has run smoothly and is presently being evaluated by Quality Control for application on the old A and B lines.

Subsequent developments at Gale will be presented in the form in which the information was actually communicated.* For our purposes, it will be most interesting to examine these events from the point of view of the General Manager of the Padlock Division and those functional managers reporting to him: Sales, Manufacturing, and Quality Control. The date today is Tuesday, July 20, 1965.

March 10, 1965

MEMORANDUM TO: Manufacturing
SUBJECT: Conversion to Hot Dip

You have our concurrence on the switch from dry rub to hot dip on A and B lines, scheduled for next Monday. The tests we completed prior to the 206 changeover proved that, as long as the solution is maintained at 150°F ± 5° and frequently agitated (to prevent the graphite from settling out), a satisfactory graphite residue

---

* For those unfamiliar with padlock nomenclature:
    CORE: all locking parts contained inside the case.
    PLUG: part of the core; the cylindrical, rotating part into which the key is inserted.
    SHACKLE: the movable steel wire loop that is partially released when padlock is unlocked.

will adhere if cores are submerged at least fifteen seconds. It also helps penetration if the trays are jiggled while in the solution.

Engineering

March 24, 1965

MEMORANDUM TO: Manufacturing
SUBJECT: Shackle Rejects

Have you made any changes on the shackle operation or changed suppliers of shackle wire? Rejects due to shackle binding were up 13 percent above normal this week.

I'm writing you on this because when my new shackle-test gal called this to the attention of someone on the shackle suboperation he gave her a bit of a hard time. Whatever caused the rise in shackle rejects, I would like to suggest that someone over there needs a dressing down on his communications—especially where ladies are involved.

Quality Control

FILE COPY

March 29, 1965

MEMORANDUM TO: General Manager, Padlock Division
SUBJECT: Progress Report on 206 Line

As of the end of last week we are now meeting the 206 production schedule. Judging by the way things are running, we should have no problem continuing to do so. We had to break in some new hands on the shackle operation during the last couple of weeks, but everyone's up to quota now. Since we are now at full volume on the line, any significant increase in the schedule will either require going to three shifts or expanding our facilities.

Quality Control is still working on test standards, but this represents no problem for us since the new line runs like clockwork and produces a damn good lock.

Manufacturing

FILE COPY

April 6, 1965

MEMORANDUM TO: Quality Control
SUBJECT: Your Memo of March 24, 1965

Just wanted you to know that we've taken action on that communication problem. I'd prefer not to go into details, but I don't think you're likely to be bothered again by anything like this from our department. We appreciate your calling the matter to our attention.

As to the jump in rejects, I'm afraid that's more or less inevitable following process changes—especially during periods of expanding production like we're in now.

Manufacturing

June 1, 1965

MEMORANDUM TO: Manufacturing
SUBJECT: Congratulations!

Congratulations on your first year's 206 production. I want you to know that T. F., Jr., and I are duly impressed with the way you got this new line rolling and more recently with the production levels you've reached and held without loss of quality.

On that score, a special note is due Quality Control for continuing to see to it that Gale customers only get the good ones. That's how we keep 'em locked in on Gale!

General Manager, Padlock Division

cc: Quality Control

FILE COPY

June 3, 1965

MEMORANDUM TO: General Manager, Padlock Division
SUBJECT: Conversion to Hot Dip

Apparently promoting Susy MacDonald to Quality Control last March had a good effect all around. Marge Jensen, for example, was always considered marginal on lubrication, but since she's had it all to herself with the new hot-dip procedure, she's going great guns. The men down in plating tell me Marge is always ready for them when they bring up the core trays. I checked with Marge herself recently and her only comment was, "No sweat!"

I go into this because I think it's high time we converted to hot dip on A and B lines. I don't know why Quality Control is dragging its feet on this one. Every day we dry-rub is just more dollars down the drain!

Manufacturing

July 8, 1965

MEMORANDUM TO: Manufacturing and Quality Control
SUBJECT: Customer Complaints of Frozen Locks

Gentlemen, something has gone very wrong with our new padlock line. We've been getting a lot of customer complaints to the effect that our locks freeze up and can't be opened unless penetrating oil is used. From what I've been able to gather, the plugs won't turn—even when enough force is exerted to break off the key. In other cases they claim they can't even get the key all the way into the plug.

I won't insult you with any theories as to what's causing this problem but I will offer this observation: There'll be more than one kind of Gale around here if this isn't cleared up—like now!

I'll forward our estimates on replacement requirements as soon as we have more specific information on the extent of the problem.

Sales

FILE COPY

July 12, 1965

MEMORANDUM TO: Sales
SUBJECT: 206 Complaints

I'm very sorry to learn about your problem. Fortunately, I can assure you that everything is running smoothly in manufacturing—so much so that I certainly hope these complaints get nailed before any of my people hear about it. We've had quite a struggle getting up to schedule on the new line, and the last thing I need is an investigation!

Incidentally, I do happen to know that shipping made some changes in packaging a month or so ago as part of our campaign to cut costs. This might bear investigation. Then there's always an outside chance that Quality Control let a few rough ones past. I doubt this, but we always have—and probably always will have—variability in the shackle fit due to variations in metallurgical characteristics of the raw shackle wire.

                                                            Manufacturing

GALE LOCKS

Gale Locks, Inc., produces a variety of doorlocks, padlocks, small safes, and other security devices. Through its padlock division, Gale has enjoyed the lion's share of the national padlock market for half a century. Simple, sturdy design, plus meticulous quality control have earned Gale a reputation for reliability and durability. This quality image plus the universal public awareness of Gale as "the biggest and oldest lockmaker in the business" are considered the major reasons for Gale's ability to hold higher prices and continue to build market share over the years.

During the last decade, however, competition has intensified. Several smaller manufacturers have produced padlocks of practically identical appearance to Gale's, but priced 20 to 40 percent lower. While relatively few hardware stores or locksmiths have discontinued the Gale lines, almost all outlets have taken on one or more competitive lines with the result that Gale sales in both its padlock lines have been affected. For three years, until about a year ago, the growth rate went into sharp decline in spite of massive advertising campaigns and sales contests—both of which represented quite a depar-

ture for the old firm. Another blow has been the advent of supermarkets and discount houses as an outlet for hardware items, including padlocks. Hardly any of these new outlets have taken on the Gale lines.

For several years Gale marketing and sales pleaded for a third new line that would be price competitive with the padlocks sold at discount houses. Until recently, top management resisted on grounds that the Gale image would be damaged and their quality lines would suffer. However, when T. Frothingham Gale, Jr., took over the reins from "Old Frothy" eighteen months ago, one of his first directives was to set up a new, low-priced padlock. As anticipated by Marketing and Sales, this new line—very similar in appearance to Gale's "middle-priced" line and bearing the Gale monogram—exceeded expectations during its first year on the market. Furthermore, sales of the new line have not, as yet, had any visible effect on the two higher-priced lines.

Manufacturing procedure for padlocks varies with quality. Gale buys the brass case for its A line (top-quality padlock) from an outside manufacturer. The lock cores (all internal locking parts) are machined from raw brass stock, rubbed with dry graphite for permanent lubrication, assembled into the cases together with the shackles (steel wire shaped in a die), and riveted in place with two pins. The padlocks are then polished, sprayed with clear lacquer, stamped with the Gale monogram, the monogram letters are paint-filled, and the finished lock is packaged.

Gale makes its own B line cases. Extruded brass bar stock is cut off, drilled, and completely machined in a Kingsbury machine. The remainder of the B line procedure is the same as the A line—the primary difference between the two lines being the greater weight and strength of the A line locks. (Each line comes in two sizes.)

The new 206 (also two sizes) is a zinc die-cast padlock. In sequence, the procedures are casting, broaching, drilling, finishing (buffing followed by anticorrosion nickel-chrome plating), assembling (core and steel wire shackle into the case), silver painting, and packaging.

The primary bottleneck in the A and B lines was always the individual rubbing of lock cores in dry graphite. In order to achieve the much greater volume required of the 206 line, a new method of lubrication has been developed by Engineering: the lock cores are left in their large tray holders, used in plating, dipped in a heated solution containing graphite in suspension, and then conveyed through an oven that bakes the residue of graphite onto the core surfaces. This eliminates individual handling of each lock core and realizes a significant labor savings. The new procedure has run smoothly and is presently being evaluated by Quality Control for application on the old A and B lines.

Subsequent developments at Gale will be presented in the form in which the information was actually communicated.* For our purposes, it will be most interesting to examine these events from the point of view of the General Manager of the Padlock Division and those functional managers reporting to him: Sales, Manufacturing, and Quality Control. The date today is Tuesday, July 20, 1965.

FILE COPY

February 12, 1965

MEMORANDUM TO: Personnel
SUBJECT: Help Wanted

I want to put in writing what I spoke to you about earlier this week: Our work load is reaching the point where I'm becoming concerned about the possibility of marginal items getting out into

---

* For those unfamiliar with padlock nomenclature:

CORE: all locking parts contained inside the case.

PLUG: part of the core; the cylindrical, rotating part into which the key is inserted.

SHACKLE: the movable steel wire loop that is partially released when padlock is unlocked.

customers' hands. As you know, our head count hasn't changed since September and our load—thanks to the 206—certainly has!

I hope you will place top priority on finding us an additional man qualified to check shackles, cores, and keys on 206s. This is our biggest bind right now, and it is a critical area for the whole division in view of our dependence on the new line.

Quality Control

FILE COPY

March 19, 1965

MEMORANDUM TO: General Manager, Padlock Division
SUBJECT: Revision of Test Procedures

We are currently revising our procedures on the shackle tolerance test. Shackle bending has always been a critical area, due to variations in skin hardness and age of wire. Final adjustments (tapping, pinching, spreading) are often required and take considerable operator skill.

Since any defect in shackle fit has a direct effect on lock function, we have decided to go from 10 percent to a 25 percent sampling on shackle test for at least the next quarter. We're going to try to accomplish this without an increase in personnel; but if this proves to be impossible, we feel the additional cost will be justified. Gale has been built on a foundation of quality, and we're not about to let anybody undermine that!

Quality Control

March 10, 1965

MEMORANDUM TO: Quality Control
SUBJECT: Your Request of February 12, 1965

We regret that we have not, as yet, been able to find a qualified candidate for the position you need to fill. Job applicants from the outside just haven't come anywhere near your specifications.

Internally, the 206 success has put everyone in pretty much the same position. However, we anticipate that certain process changes

planned in Manufacturing might make it possible for them to release one or two people. If this occurs, you are at the top of our
list. Such a person, with a little intensive training on your part,
ought to fill the bill.

Personnel

FILE COPY

March 24, 1965

MEMORANDUM TO: Manufacturing
SUBJECT: Shackle Rejects

Have you made any changes on the shackle operation or changed
suppliers of shackle wire? Rejects due to shackle binding were up 13
percent above normal this week.

I'm writing you on this because when my new shackle-test gal
called this to the attention of someone on the shackle suboperation
he gave her a bit of a hard time. Whatever caused the rise in shackle rejects, I would like to suggest that someone over there needs a
dressing down on his communications—especially where ladies are
involved.

Quality Control

April 6, 1965

MEMORANDUM TO: Quality Control
SUBJECT: Your Memo of March 24, 1965

Just wanted you to know that we've taken action on that communication problem. I'd prefer not to go into details, but I don't think
you're likely to be bothered again by anything like this from our
department. We appreciate your calling the matter to our attention.

As to the jump in rejects, I'm afraid that's more or less inevitable
following process changes—especially during periods of expanding
production like we're in now.

Manufacturing

<u>FILE COPY</u>

June 1, 1965

MEMORANDUM TO: Manufacturing
SUBJECT: Congratulations!

Congratulations on your first year's 206 production. I want you to know that T. F., Jr., and I are duly impressed with the way you got this new line rolling and more recently with the production levels you've reached and held without loss of quality.

On that score, a special note is due Quality Control for continuing to see to it that Gale customers only get the good ones. That's how we keep 'em locked in on Gale!

General Manager, Padlock Division

cc: Quality Control

July 8, 1965

MEMORANDUM TO: Manufacturing and <u>Quality Control</u>
SUBJECT: Customer Complaints of <u>Frozen Locks</u>

Gentlemen, something has gone very wrong with our new padlock line. We've been getting a lot of customer complaints to the effect that our locks freeze up and can't be opened unless penetrating oil is used. From what I've been able to gather, the plugs won't turn—even when enough force is exerted to break off the key. In other cases they claim they can't even get the key all the way into the plug.

I won't insult you with any theories as to what's causing this problem but I will offer this observation: There'll be more than one kind of Gale around here if this isn't cleared up—like now!

I'll forward our estimates on replacement requirements as soon as we have more specific information on the extent of the problem.

Sales

July 15, 1965

MEMORANDUM TO: Quality Control
SUBJECT: Susy MacDonald

How is Susy making· out? We in Personnel had some misgivings about her ability to grasp Quality Control sampling and testing procedures, but she was the best girl on the dry-rub operation so when they converted to the new hot-dip procedure four months ago we felt Susy had to be given first chance at the promotion to your test group.

Please give us feedback on Susy. Her promotion represents sort of a test case for the new policy of giving top performers first shot at a better job regardless of the type of work involved.

Personnel

FILE COPY

July 19, 1965

MEMORANDUM TO: Personnel
SUBJECT: Susy MacDonald

Susy's doing great. As you may recall, we took her on because of our projected expansion on shackle test. Once she was broken in, we upped the sample; and judging by results, Susy's got a sharp eye. We're very pleased with her performance to date. As a matter of fact, it now looks like she may have helped nip a major problem in the bud.

Quality Control

The Solution

Gale Deviation Analysis

1. *List deviations:*
   - *a.* Growing competition
   - *b.* Price-cutting, affecting A and B sales
   - *c.* Rising materials costs (Krinland)
   - *d.* Production of rejects (caught by Quality Control)
   - *e.* Delay in conversion to hot dip on A and B
   - *f.* Conflicting views on Gale product strategy
   - *g.* Complaints of locks freezing up
   - *h.* Korvette buyer threatening to switch
   - *i.* Excessive rejects due to shackle binding

j. Poor communications: Quality Control versus Manufacturing

k. Personnel questioning management policy

l. Quality Control shorthanded on 206 line

Did you and your team find all these deviations? If not, it may be that you were trying to do two jobs at once: listing deviations *and* searching for possible causes. This tends to focus your attention on one problem to the exclusion of others.

2. *Set priorities:* In my opinion, the *urgency* and *potential consequences* of the customer complaints about freezing locks clearly makes this first order of business for the general manager at Gale.

3. *Define the deviation:*

Customer Complaints of Freezing Locks

Reported	*Not reported*
ITEM: New 206	A or B line
Plugs won't turn	shackle trouble
Can't insert key	any other problems
SOURCE: Customers, yachtsman, dealers	Quality Control, Manufacturing, etc.
PLACE: Stamford, Charleston, Los Angeles, Seattle	Midwest or any other locations
TIME: Beginning July	Prior to end June
	Prior years
	After penetrating oil added
AMOUNT: Snowed with complaints	
Several dealers	
Mounting	Level or decreasing

4. *Identify differences:* Differences between the 206 and both the A and B lines:

- cheaper
- different material
- different production process
- different personnel
- new hot-dip lubrication

Difference between Stamford, Charleston, Los Angeles, and Seattle as opposed to the Midwest: all four are Coastal areas, with higher salt content in the air.

Possible difference between beginning July and prior months: vacations and generally increased outdoor activity.

5. *Identify changes:* All changes in the 206 except one occurred about one year ago, when the lock was introduced. This one was the new hot-dip lubrication method introduced about the middle of March. Note that the new method requires fairly strict adherence to procedures and is "manned" by Marge, a somewhat casual sounding worker considered marginal in some respects.

6. *Note possible causes:* By now it fairly leaps at you: the new lubrication may be inadequate (possibly due to Marge's performance), causing locks to freeze up.

Other possibilities are the different material and processes of the new 206.

Still another possibility is that the 206 just can't stand up to a heavy salt atmosphere.

7. *Logical test of possible causes:* If it were the materials or processes, why no complaints until July? (The 206 has been out for a year.)

If the new lubrication were the sole cause, why no complaints from other areas?

If the 206 won't work in a salt atmosphere, why no complaints from Coastal areas until almost a year after the lock was introduced to the market?

Thus it looks like a *combination* cause of inadequate lubrication *plus* salt atmosphere. This hypothesis fits with all the information in the definition of the deviation.

8. *Operating test of probable cause:* This would be expensive and actually has already been done (though inadvertently). We now know that 206s lubricated by the new hot-dip process were sent everywhere (since April) and that failures

have been reported only from Coastal areas. We know that earlier 206s, lubricated by the dry-rub method, did not produce complaints. We also know that additional lubrication (by penetrating oil) fixed a frozen 206 lock.

9. *Develop alternatives:*

■ Train Marge
■ Back to dry-rub
■ Don't sell 206s on the Coasts
■ Enclose penetrating oil
■ Drop the 206 line

10. *Evaluate alternatives:* You lack sufficient information in the exercise to do an adequate job of this. Actual costs, sales projections, etc., would be needed. You could, however, have indicated the specific kinds of information you would need in order to make an effective evaluation of action alternatives.

Evaluate Your Process

If you were able to record your discussions, now is the time to listen to the tape. As you listen, try to answer these questions:

■ How efficient were we?
■ Did we have a plan for our work together?
■ How well did we follow it?
■ Did the general manager maintain control?
■ How did he do it?
■ Were the others contributing effectively?
■ Did we miss important points? Why?
■ What would we do differently in the future?

For a more complete and analytical review of your team discussion, apply the discussion analysis technique outlined in Chapter 3. Now, however, since your task was deviation analysis, the headings would be different:

DISCUSSION ANALYSIS SHEET

	Listing problems	Setting priorities	Defining a deviation	Differences and changes	Possible causes	Proposing actions
T						
I						
M						
E						
.						
.						
.						
.						

As you listen, put a check under the heading that best describes each comment you hear, moving down one notch for each notation. The record should help you evaluate how orderly you were and should help you decide what additional controls you would want to apply in the future. If the bulk of your checks more or less form a diagonal pattern across from the upper left to lower right on the Discussion Analysis Sheet, your team followed an unusually orderly process. Most groups, on their first try, find a lot of jumping back and forth from left to right at all levels on the sheet. This suggests that the discussion was either following some other plan or no plan at all.

Now you're ready to try it on a real one. Good luck!

Notes:
Related Readings

1. Pavlov, I. P., *Conditioned Reflexes*, London: Oxford University Press, 1927.
2. Thorndike, E. L., *Human Learning*, New York: Century Company, 1931.
3. Ebbinghaus, H., *Memory*, New York: Teachers College, Columbia University, 1913.
4. Allport, G. W., *Personality: A Psychological Interpretation*, New York: Henry Holt and Company, Inc., 1937.
5. Köhler, W., *Gestalt Psychology*, New York: Liveright Publishing Corporation, 1929.
6. Herzberg, F., *The Motivation To Work*, 2d ed., New York: John Wiley & Sons, Inc., 1967.
7. Maslow, A. H., *Motivation and Personality*, New York: Harper and Row Publishers, Inc., 1954.
8. Drucker, P. F., *The Age of Discontinuity*, New York: Harper and Row Publishers, Inc., 1968.

9. Dale, E., *Management, Theory and Practice,* New York: McGraw-Hill Book Company, 1965.
10. Barnard, C. I., *The Functions Of The Executive,* Cambridge, Mass.: Harvard University Press, 1938.
11. Drucker, P. F., *The Practice of Management,* New York: Harper and Row Publishers, Inc., 1954.
12. Metcalf, H. C. and L. Urwick, *Dynamic Administration,* New York: Harper & Brothers, 1940.
13. Kepner, C. H. and B. B. Tregoe, *The Rational Manager,* New York: McGraw-Hill Book Company, 1965.
14. Maier, N. R. F., "A New Approach to Leadership Principles for Problem Solving Conferences," *Michigan Business Review,* June, 1962.
15. Dooher, J. and V. Marquis, *Effective Communication On The Job,* New York: American Management Association, 1956.
16. Lippitt, R. and R. White, "An Experimental Study of Leadership and Group Life," in Newcomb et al., *Readings in Social Psychology,* New York: Henry Holt and Company, Inc., 1952.
17. Emery, D. A., "Managerial Leadership Through Motivation by Objectives," *Personnel Psychology,* vol. 12, no. 1, Spring, 1959.
18. Blake, R. R. and J. S. Mouton, *The Managerial Grid,* Houston, Tex.: Gulf Publishing Company, 1964.
19. Gregory, C. E., *The Management of Intelligence,* New York: McGraw-Hill Book Company, 1967.
20. Osborn, A. F., *Applied Imagination,* New York: Charles Scribner's Sons, 1957.
21. Gordon, J. J. and G. M. Prince, *The Operational Mechanisms of Synectics,* Cambridge, Mass.: Synectics, Inc., 1960.
22. Maslow, A. H., "Emotional Blocks to Creativity," *Journal of Individual Psychology,* vol. 14, pp. 51–56, 1958.
23. Lewin, K., *A Dynamic Theory of Personality,* New York: McGraw-Hill Book Company, 1935, chap. IV.
24. Leighton, A. H., *The Governing of Men,* Princeton, N.J.: Princeton University Press, 1946.
25. Nichols, R. C. and L. A. Stevens, *Are You Listening?* New York: McGraw-Hill Book Company, 1957.

Index

Index